Portraits of Perseverance

PORTRAITS OF
PERSEVERANCE

Henry Gariepy

VICTOR BOOKS ®

A DIVISION OF SCRIPTURE PRESS PUBLICATIONS INC.
USA CANADA ENGLAND

Unless otherwise noted, Scripture quotations are from the
Holy Bible, New International Version, © *1973, 1978, 1984,*
International Bible Society. Used by permission of Zondervan
Bible Publishers. Other quotations are from The New King
James Version (NKJV). © *1979, 1980, 1982, Thomas Nelson,*
Inc., Publishers; the Authorized (King James) Version (KJV);
and The Amplified Bible Old Testament *(AMP),* © *1962, 1964*
by Zondervan Publishing House.

This special Billy Graham Evangelistic Association edition is
published with permission from the original publisher, Victor
Books, Wheaton, Illinois.

Recommended Dewey Decimal Classification: 248.3
Suggested Subject Headings: DEVOTIONAL; JOB
Library of Congress Catalog Card Number: 89-60145
ISBN: 0-89693-704-6

Contents

*Dedicated to
Our Grandchildren*

*Dawn
Sarah
Stephen
Lauren
Kathryn
Elizabeth
Alison
Jonathan
Carissa
Brian*

and others who may come

Introduction

The Book of Job is every man's story. It is not merely to be read or studied; it is to be experienced. Each of us is engaged in a life-and-death struggle with the forces of evil. Each of us either has had or will have a rendezvous with trial and severe testing. The drama of Job is a mirror reflecting our own deep needs and struggle.

Job suffered the greatest calamities of anyone in the Bible. His whole world came tumbling down, and he reached the nadir of human experience. But, above all, the Book of Job is one of triumph. We see, in the trial of Job, the marvelous grace of God that brings blessing out of brokenness, celebration out of calamity, triumph out of tragedy.

The reader of Job will not find glib answers to the problem of suffering and evil in the world. But the diligent and devout reader will find a perspective that enables him to see through suffering, to go from the "why" to the "who" which sustains and enables the believer to triumph over his trial.

Serendipities of rich insights and inspiration await the serious reader of Job. Its lofty eloquence renders it one of the most engrossing readings in all of literature.

Golden texts add luster to the pages and to the believer's experience. With Job we too may attest, "He knows the way that I take; when He has tested me, I will come forth as gold" (Job 23:10). We will hear from these pages the sublime song

God gave to Job in the night, the song that has sung its way into the hearts of believers around the world: "I know that my Redeemer lives" (19:25). From the lips of Elihu, we will hear sage advice for our full-throttle lifestyle and the fury and frenzy of our world: "Stop and consider God's wonders" (37:14).

We will encounter an unsurpassed moment of Old Testament testimony as Job stakes his destiny on the living Redeemer who "in the end . . . will stand upon the earth" (19:25). We will witness the turning point of Job's experience when he takes the quantum leap from hearsay to a firsthand experience with God. And we will encounter the longest recorded discourse with God as in unsurpassed poetic beauty He cites the ravishing mystery, might, and magnificence of His creation. His discourse assures His providence and care and is garnished with the intrigue and rare revelation of the humor of God.

Job is a multifaceted, multi-splendored book. *Portraits of Perseverance* selects the textual gems of this great book that sparkle with insights and inspiration. Included are facets of timeless truths from some of the lesser-known texts. Fasten your seat belt. You are in for an exciting, exhilarating, and rewarding adventure in the Word and will of God.

Portrait One
THE REAL JOB

There lived a man whose name was Job (Job 1:1).

Was Job a real person? Or is his story a parable? Are Job and his story real events in the history of man, or is he a mythical character, a clever invention to answer the greatest riddle of humanity?

As often is the case, the Bible gives its own best answers to the questions it raises. First, the Bible testifies to the inspiration of its record: "All Scripture is God-breathed" (2 Tim. 3:16). The Christian believes the Bible is the inspired Word of God. Jesus affirmed the Old Testament Scripture as God's Word to man (Matt. 22:29-31). Thus we accept the simple and straightforward opening statement: "There lived a man whose name was Job."

God Himself attests that Job was real, holding him in high reputation with Noah and Daniel (Ezek. 14:14, 20). In the New Testament, James refers to Job as a paragon of patience (James 5:11). And Job is quoted in Romans 11:35 (Job 41:11) and in 1 Corinthians 3:19 (Job 5:13).

Endorsed by unimpeachable biblical testimony, Job was a real person. We are not studying a mythical character, but one who battled the trials of life, one who experienced heartbreak and loss, one who felt the agony of pain, one who knew the depths of loneliness and despair, one who endured the hurt of misunderstanding and rebuke. Because the person and story of Job are true, this book has an authentic message for us.

The land of Uz is somewhere outside of Palestine. This non-Israelitish element gives universalism to the book. It is not bound by Hebrew tradition. The term for God's name in the poetic colloquy is the non-Hebrew *Elohim*, not the Jewish term *Yahweh*, enhancing its universal appeal.

Each of us identifies with Job. We have an affinity with his contest and trials. Praise God, we can also identify with his triumph of faith!

> *Our Father, in our world of change and deception, thank You for the credibility of Your Word, the eternal trustworthiness of its teachings and truths.*

Portrait Two

FOUNDATION OF FAITH

This man was blameless and upright; he feared God and shunned evil (Job 1:1).

The first five verses give a revealing profile of Job.

His faith is depicted: "This man was blameless and upright; he feared God and shunned evil." The Bible scholar Delitzsch defines the word *blameless* as denoting "the whole heart disposed toward God and what is good, and also well-disposed toward mankind."

His righteousness and integrity were attested by God (1:8), by his wife (2:9) (which is always a good test of a man's character), and by his own inward witness of integrity that sustained him in his trials and against false accusation. Job was, before others and God, a model man.

Faith was the foundation for Job's life. It was because he had faith in God and his life was guided by that faith that he endured the calamities and great test of his life.

When trial or tragedy strikes, it is what we have been before that determines how we will react. When the storms of adversity beat on us, it will be the foundations of our life that will sustain and enable us to endure. As with Job, so faith and righteousness will decide the outcome of life's testings. Ella Wheeler Wilcox (*Masterpieces of Religious Verse*, Harper & Brothers, 1948) has expressed this truth in memorable verse:

> One ship drives east and another drives west
> With the selfsame winds that blow.

'Tis the set of the sails
And not the gales
Which tells us the way to go.

Like the winds of the sea are the ways of fate,
   As we voyage along through life:
   'Tis the set of a soul
   That decides the goal,
   And not the calm or the strife.

*Lord, increase my faith so that my life will have a foundation
that will stand the testings and trials that will surely come.*

Portrait Three

FAMILY PRIORITY

Early in the morning he would offer a burnt offering for each of them (Job 1:5).

In this five-verse profile of Job, not only is his faith depicted, but his family is described. He had seven sons and three daughters. We are given a picture of joyful, harmonious family gatherings with sons rotating hospitality and the daughters invited.

Job was a priest as well as father to his family, fulfilling the ritual offerings on behalf of his children. It was not sporadic, for we read, "This was Job's regular custom" (1:5). He was concerned that his children be free of sin and in right standing with God. Job is a good example for those who think they can transfer to the church or to others a responsibility for the spiritual training and character of their children.

In David's tragic loss of his son Absalom, we hear his poignant cry: "Would God I had died for thee" (2 Sam. 18:33). His lament for his son would not have been wrung from his lips if he could have said, "Would God I had lived for thee." It was an example of too little too late. Our children need our example and training from their earliest years and throughout life. All too soon that little girl in the frilly white dress grows up to be a young woman in blue jeans. And that boy who is taking more cues from us than we will ever know will soon be a man.

U.S. Senate Chaplain Richard Halverson once prayed before that august assembly: "Forgive those of us who give family such a low priority. . . . Help the Senators not to be so busy trying to save the nation that they let their children go to hell." For we who are parents, our children and family are our most sacred priority.

Job was faithful as a priest to his family. May we, as he, be regular in our devotion to the spiritual needs of our family. May we, as Job, make "sacrifices" for their spiritual good. Let us be counted faithful in life's most sacred relationship and responsibility.

Heavenly Father, thank You for my family. How precious and sacred they are. Help me to be a faithful example and diligent in my spiritual responsibilities to them.

Portrait Four

FORTUNE AND FAME

He was the greatest man among all the people of the East (Job 1:3).

Not only is Job's faith depicted, his family described, but in his profile we find his fortune is detailed. Job's land, livestock, and servants would have given him a prominent listing in Dunn & Bradstreet. He was fabulously wealthy. His portfolio included 7,000 sheep, 3,000 camels, 500 yoke of oxen, 500 donkeys, and a large number of servants.

Fortune and possessions have become obsessions with many in our materialistic society today. There are too many who know "the price of everything and the value of nothing." We can become so glutted with luxuries that we lose the art of enjoying life's essentials. Having what money can buy, let us not lose the beautiful things money cannot buy. Let us beware of the danger of "affluenza" that is epidemic around us. The Russian writer, Aleksandr Solzhenitsyn, writing of the hard lessons he learned in the Gulag prison camp, shared that one of his major discoveries for survival was to "keep as few things as possible . . . to let memory be my travel bag."

Finally, in Job's profile we have his fame denoted. His fame spread throughout that part of the world. "He was the greatest man among all the people of the East" (1:3). This ancient Titan of the East was renowned and his name proverbial for fortune and integrity. He was a "legend in his own time."

But fame is a fleeting and fickle mistress. Its laurels fade all too soon, its honors grow dim. Poet Emily Dickinson reminds us, "Fame is a fickle food. . . . Men eat of it and die."

In a book long out of print was an illustration of people reaching up to grasp bubbles floating in the air with such labels as riches, fame, pleasures, honors, etc. Below the picture was the caption: "Vain efforts theirs who try to overtake the bubbles which if caught would break."

Fame and fortune are fragile bubbles of life. As with Job, they can easily be burst under life's turn of events. But, as with Job, we can hold on to faith which can be ours through eternity.

Precious Lord, help me to discern between life's tinsel and its treasures, the ephemeral and the eternal, the transient and the timeless, and to lay hold on eternal life through Jesus Christ my Lord.

Portrait Five
OUR ADVERSARY

Satan—the adversary and accuser—also came among them
(Job 1:6, AMP).

Following the brief profile of Job, we are suddenly carried
aloft into the courts of heaven. We are ushered into one of the
most extraordinary scenes of the Bible and made privy to the
plot of the great drama to unfold.

Angels present themselves to God. These heavenly beings,
God's servants and couriers, slip in and out of the Bible narrative from Genesis to Revelation.

But we must confess surprise to find Satan in attendance.
Here he is quite different from Milton's fallen angel, Lucifer,
son of the morning, who was as the "sun shorn of his
beams." Satan here is presented as a vagabond spirit and one
whose name literally means "adversary." He is called to account by God, the Sovereign of the universe.

Satan is the deadly adversary of every man. Jesus identified
him as "a murderer from the beginning" (John 8:44). Peter,
who knew firsthand the devil's wiles and power, warns,
"Your enemy the devil prowls around like a roaring lion looking for someone to devour" (1 Peter 5:8).

Satan is real and powerful and seeks to destroy each of us.
We need to take him seriously. C.S. Lewis cautions in his
preface to *The Screwtape Letters* (Collins): "There are two equal
and opposite errors into which our race can fall about the
devils. One is to disbelieve in their existence. The other is to
believe, and to feel an excessive and unhealthy interest in them."

Don't ever trust the cease-fires of Satan. He will surely tempt and test you and try to destroy your faith. Just as as he was Job's deadly adversary, so he is the archenemy of your soul. Our Lord, in the wilderness temptations, gives us the secret of victory by responding to him with the Word of God: "It is written."

With Job and the songwriter, we too may find that "Jehovah is our strength. . . . In vain does Satan then oppose, For God is stronger than His foes."

Almighty God, help me to realize that I have a powerful adversary who seeks to destroy my soul. May I ever have power and victory through the Holy Spirit's presence and power within me.

Portrait Six
A STORM IS COMING

Then Satan went out from the presence of the Lord (Job 1:12).

We will soon see the classic example of "when bad things happen to good people."

In our text, when "Satan went out from the presence of the Lord," it was to attack Job and try to destroy his faith. Be assured he will also aggressively try to destroy each of us.

So, if today the sun shines brightly and life flows along like a song, be prepared. The storm that is brewing will unleash its fury and will try our faith as by fire. As we journey with the man from Uz, we will discover faith that survives fire.

Ella Wheeler Wilcox (*Masterpieces of Religion*, Harper & Brothers, 1948) reminds us, in the context of our Lord's experience, that there awaits each of us a time of testing and trial:

In golden youth when seems the earth,
A summer-land of singing mirth,
When souls are glad and hearts are light,
And not a shadow lurks in sight,
We do not know it, but there lies,
Somewhere veiled under evening skies,
A garden which we all must see—
The Garden of Gethsemane.

With joyous steps we go our ways,
Love lends a halo to our days;

Light sorrows sail like clouds afar,
We laugh and say how glad we are.
We hurry on; and hurrying, go
Close to the border-land of woe;
That waits for you, and waits for me
Forever waits Gethsemane.

All those who journey, soon or late,
Must pass within the garden's gate;
Must kneel alone in darkness there,
And battle with some fierce despair.
God pity those who cannot say,
"Not mine, but Thine," who only pray,
"Let this cup pass," and cannot see
The purpose in Gethsemane.

*God, our Refuge and our Strength, help me today to build up
the resources of my faith so when it shall be tried by fire, it will
endure and I will be more than conqueror.*

Portrait Seven

PROSPERITY THEOLOGY

Does Job fear God for nothing? (Job 1:9)

The Lord said to Satan, "Have you considered My servant, Job? There is no one on earth like him; he is blameless and upright, a man who fears God and shuns evil" (1:8). In contrast to God's enthusiastic commendation, Satan scoffed: "Does Job fear God for nothing?" (1:9)

The Book of Job revolves around the challenge of this pivotal question. It probes the motivation of our righteousness and service to God. Satan's cynical answer implies love and loyalty to God is bought, that there is no righteousness without reward. Satan charged that God had put a hedge around Job; He had protected and blessed him. "Take away his prosperity and his righteousness will turn to cursing," challenged Satan.

God accepted Satan's challenge with a permission and a prohibition. He was given permission to do anything to Job's possessions but prohibited to touch his person.

Satan blatantly charged that Job's righteousness was linked with his prosperity. It is not uncommon to hear a prosperity theology preached today, especially via the electronic church. Well-known media preachers proclaim that God's will for Christians is to enjoy prosperity and health as a result of their faith. And there are those who teach that through visualization, success can be achieved. The New Age Movement embraces Prosperity Theology as its claim to bring in the Millennium without the Messiah.

The challenge Satan flung out against Job is one that tests our own motivation. Do we serve God for nothing? Do we serve Him not for the benefits but for the blessing of His love, not for His gifts but because of His grace, not for the things of this earth but for the treasures of heaven?

May we say with the songwriter, Edward Joy:

> What to me are all the joys of earth?
>   What to me is every sight I see,
> Save the sight of Thee, O Friend of mine?
>   Jesus, Thou art everything to me.

Eternal God, purify my motivation that I will serve You out of love and gratitude for Yourself and Your boundless grace to me.

FAITH AMID THE STORM

In all this, Job did not sin by charging God with wrongdoing (Job 1:22).

An avalanche of woes now thundered on Job in all its fury. First, a lone survivor appeared from a terrorist raid, informing Job that his oxen and donkeys had been taken and his servants massacred.

Even as this report was given, the second stroke of misfortune was announced by another survivor who told of sheep and servants killed by lightning. In rapid sequence, another survivor told of the capture of Job's prized camels and the killing of the servants. Three times, without intermission, there was the recital of worsened catastrophes. The adversary wanted to break Job's resistance before he had time to recover.

Job may well have turned to his wife and said, "We've lost all our possessions, but at least we still have that which is most precious—our children and family." Just then, a messenger came with the worst news of all: "Your children are all dead, killed when a whirlwind collapsed the house where they were feasting." Such words strike as a sharp arrow in the tender heart of an unsuspecting parent. In one shattering moment, ten vibrant, beautiful lives ceased to be. The loss of his offspring also left Job without posterity, considered a tragedy in the Eastern world.

And the richest man in the East was suddenly, in successive strokes of calamity, stripped of possessions and family. He lost everything. He was ruined.

In the ritual of grief common to the Oriental world of that time, Job tore off his robe and shaved his head to signify his glory was now gone. Bankruptcy and ten fresh graves—we ask, How can anyone survive such a crucible of calamities? And lurking on the sidelines was Satan, waiting now for Job to curse God for such undeserved violence.

In this moment, Job fell to the ground, not in depression, despair, or defeat, but rather "in worship." He said, "Naked I came from my mother's womb, and naked I will depart. The Lord gave and the Lord has taken away; may the name of the Lord be praised" (1:20-21).

And it is recorded, "In all this, Job did not sin by charging God with wrongdoing" (1:22). Job survived the storm. His faith stood firm. He had victory in this first dramatic combat with Satan.

When the great testing or trial comes on our lives, with John Greenleaf Whittier from his "The Eternal Goodness," we may affirm:

> I know not where His islands lift
>   Their fronded palms in air;
> I only know I cannot drift
>   Beyond His love and care. . . .

> And thou, O Lord! by whom are seen
>   Thy creatures as they be,
> Forgive me if too close I lean
>   My human heart on Thee!

God of love, when dark shadows cross the threshold of my life, illumine my path by the One who is my Light and Salvation.

Portrait Nine
HOLDING ON TO INTEGRITY

Are you still holding on to your integrity? (Job 2:9)

"Are you still holding on to your integrity?" was the challenge sarcastically flung at Job by his wife. It is the same challenge that comes to us in our testings and trials.

Are we holding on to our integrity when the tempter comes at us with his subtle strategies and temptations to defeat us? Are we holding on to our integrity when the storms of life blow fiercely on us? Are we holding on to our integrity when it may seem we are standing all alone against the wiles of Satan? Are we holding on to our integrity when it doesn't seem to pay to do what's right? This question poses a pivotal challenge for each of us.

In February 1985, Billy Graham spoke about integrity as he addressed some 4,000 Christian media leaders. The renowned evangelist was held in profound respect by those of us gathered there. His character and reputation have been irreproachable with never a question about his finances, marriage, or morality. Yet this man of impeccable character and leadership shared with us his great concern: "The thing I fear more than anything else in the world is that I may make a mistake and bring disrepute on the Gospel, and my power be taken away and I become a castaway. Rather than anything else on my tombstone, I would want to have inscribed the testimony from Proverbs, 'I have walked in my integrity.' " If Billy Graham lives with that as his great concern, how much more should we be careful and prayerful to hold on to our integrity.

"Holding on" is a good phrase because Satan will try to rob us of our integrity. It is all too easy to let integrity slip away from us, to exchange it for the phantom charms of the world, to compromise it for the enticements of Satan. The secret of success in the Christian life may very well be summed up as "holding on."

Job held on to his integrity, and that is why God twice named him in the timeless trio of "Noah, Daniel, and Job" (Ezek. 14:14, 20). By holding on to our integrity, we too will have God's commendation.

Salvationist Ruth Tracy has lyricized this truth for us in song:

> I've found the secret of success,
>   'Tis holding on, 'tis holding on;
> The way to every blessedness,
>   'Tis holding on, 'tis holding on.
> Our warfare may be hard and fierce,
> Oft Satan's arrows wound and pierce,
> But still we get more smiles than tears
>   By holding on, by holding on.
>
> If full salvation you would gain,
>   Keep holding on, keep holding on;
> To conquer sins that bring you pain,
>   Keep holding on, keep holding on.
> God loves to give the better part,
> Not unto those who only start,
> But those who seek with all their heart,
>   And then in faith keep holding on.

Heavenly Father, when fierce temptations assail, when the storms test the foundations of my life, help me by Your grace to hold on to my integrity.

Portrait Ten
ACCEPTANCE

Shall we accept good from God, and not trouble? (Job 2:10)

The diabolical strategy of Satan is seen in the crescendo of blows he inflicted on Job—disaster, divestiture, death, disease, desertion. His cunning is employed against every child of God as he seeks to destroy our faith.

Job's wife here makes her first of two appearances. With her husband, she had suffered the loss of their property and children. She had watched Job become ravaged by hideous disease. She could stand it no longer and taunted, "Are you still holding on to your integrity? Curse God and die!" (2:9)

Job labeled his wife's advice as "foolish." He did not condemn her but sought to help her keep a spiritual perspective, saying, "Shall we accept good from God, and not trouble?" And in this ultimate test, Job's faith survived: "In all this, Job did not sin in what he said" (2:10).

Job's word "accept" is a clue to his survival and triumph. Acceptance is a watershed we reach in suffering and trial. We prefer to resist it, fight it, deny it, escape it. Elizabeth Kubler-Ross, in her book, *On Death and Dying,* has elucidated the five successive stages people go through as they face their impending death: denial, anger, bargaining, depression, and acceptance. The last and ultimate stage is acceptance. Only then are they really prepared for death.

Elisabeth Elliot, in 1956, lost her missionary husband in the Auca Indian massacre in the jungles of Ecuador. With her small daughter, Valerie, she went into the very village of tribesmen who had killed her husband. There she ministered and saw God's miracles. From this experience, she writes:

> Only in acceptance lies peace not in
> resignation nor in busyness.
> Resignation is surrender to fate.
> Acceptance is surrender to God.
> Resignation lies down quietly in an empty universe.
> Acceptance rises up to meet the God who
> fills that universe with purpose and destiny.
> Resignation says, "I can't."
> Acceptance says, "God can!"
> Resignation says, "It's all over for me."
> Acceptance asks, "Now that I am here, what's
> next, Lord?"
> Resignation says, "What a waste."
> Acceptance asks, "In what redemptive way
> will You use this mess, Lord?" (Quoted in *Lord if I Ever Needed You*, Creath Davis, Baker)

Long before Elizabeth Kubler-Ross discovered it as a key to facing death and before modern psychiatrists enunciated it as a therapy for stress, Job testified to acceptance as a means of coping with the worst that life can throw at us. Elisabeth Elliot and other contemporary Christians who have gone through deep waters also remind us that we must be ready to accept trouble as well as the good that comes to us in life.

Dear Lord, help me to be a realist, not to look at my world through rose-colored glasses but to see its clouds as well as sunshine, to be ready to accept its storms as well as welcome its fair weather.

Portrait Eleven
JOB'S COMFORTERS

*When Job's three friends . . . heard about all the troubles
that had come upon him, they set out from their
homes . . . to go . . . and comfort him (Job 2:11).*

We left Job as an outcast on a dunghill outside of town where
he sat in unrelieved adversity. His faith had survived the crescendo of trials that had taken his possessions, family, and
health. All he had left was his wife and the respect of his
friends and peers.

Our narrative next introduces us to Job's three friends who
will occupy center stage for most of the drama.

Bad news travels fast. Our anonymous author tells us that
"when Job's three friends, Eliphaz the Temanite, Bildad the
Shuhite and Zophar the Naamathite, heard about all the troubles that had come upon him, they . . . met together to go and
sympathize with him and comfort him" (2:11).

"Job's comforters" has become a disparaging term because
of their relentless imputations. But to their credit, they were
not sunshine acquaintances but friends who gathered around
the sufferer in his days of darkness.

First we are told of their sojourn. The account reads, "They
set out from their homes . . . to go and sympathize with him
and comfort him" (2:11).

Their shock is next described in detail. They were totally
unprepared for what they saw. The pasture was without livestock; the servants' quarters were deserted. And the record
tells us that when they saw Job, "they could hardly recognize
him" (2:12).

When last they saw him, he was in his regal robes and had radiance of body and spirit. It was a far cry from the shocking spectacle of a disfigured Job sitting on the dung heap. Now they must have at first mistaken him for one of the wretched beggars or lepers accustomed to being seen in that locus of outcasts. Such a gruesome sight made the three friends break forth in uncontrollable grief. They screamed, and, according to their age-old custom, tore their clothes and threw dust on their heads.

Their sadness is also depicted: "When they saw him from a distance . . . they began to weep aloud" (2:12). They genuinely grieved over the plight of their friend.

Finally, their silence dominates their response. They were shocked into silence. For seven days and seven nights they sat with Job in stunned silence. They were overwhelmed by what they saw. They sat on the ground with Job and "no one said a word to him, because they saw how great his suffering was" (2:13). They watched him writhing in pain and torment and tried to understand why such magnitude of tragedy befell him.

The writer of Proverbs reminds us, "A friend loves at all times, and a brother is born for adversity" (Prov. 17:17). How fortunate and blessed is the person who has a friend to stand with him when adversity strikes. Have we not experienced the truth of the maxim: "A joy shared is a double joy; a sorrow shared is only half a sorrow"?

Whatever our assets may be, the greatest treasure of a life will always be in its friendships. Wealthy indeed is the man who has his life enriched with friends.

Most of the Book of Job records the visit and dialogue of Job's friends. We will profit from the insights that will come to us from Job's comforters who now move to center stage. There are both positive and negative lessons to be gleaned from their lyrical lines. Though remote from us in time and culture, we will hear in their words some clear echoes of contemporary thought and theology. Eliphaz, Bildad, and Zophar have some most intriguing, interesting, and illuminating things to say to us.

Father, help me to be a cup of strength to my friends who suffer and go through trial. May I be an encourager, a comforter, an instrument of Your grace.

THE SACRAMENT OF SILENCE

No one said a word to him, because they saw how great his suffering was (Job 2:13).

Sometimes words are inappropriate, an intrusion on the deepest and most sacred experiences of life. There are times when all we can offer to one in deep sorrow is our presence and the sacrament of silence.

When Job's three friends saw his horrible plight, his calamitous losses, his disfigurement and isolation, "They sat on the ground with him for seven days and seven nights. No one said a word to him, because they saw how great his suffering was" (2:13). Seven days was the customary mourning period for the dead. His three friends grieved as though Job were dead.

The seven-day silence of Job's friends was far more eloquent than any words they could have spoken. How different it was from the Pollyanna attitude sometimes encountered in the question during difficult times, "How are you?" Suppose that his friends had asked Job, "How are you doing?" Too often there is projected the superficial theology, "Trust God and all will be all right."

Jean Fleming, in her book, *Between Walden and the Whirlwind*, reminds us: "We live in a noisy, busy world. Silence and solitude are not twentieth-century words. They fit the era of Victorian lace, high-button shoes and kerosene lamps better than our age of television, video arcades, and joggers wired with earphones. We have become a people with an aversion to quiet and an uneasiness with being alone" (p. 73, Navpress, 1985). We are so often afraid of silence. We have to fill it with words, whether we have anything to say or not.

In our world, it is the quiet forces that bring the most power. Sunbeams fall all day long on our earth, silently, unheard by human ear. Yet they bring a marvelous energy and blessing to the earth. Gravity is a silent force, no noise or rattle, yet it holds the stars and worlds in their orbits and keeps them on their courses with unvarying precision. The dew comes silently in the night and bestows life and beauty on each plant and flower. God's mightiest miracles are wrought in silence. Noise and confusion come from man. God calls us, in the words of Thomas Kelly, to "the recreating silences" as He invites us to "be still and know that I am God" (Ps. 46:10).

The seven-day silence of Job's friends has a valuable message to us in our world of sound and fury. It reminds us there are times when silence is the only appropriate response, that there is a sacrament of silence to be observed in life's most sacred moments.

Lord, help me to heed Your call to come apart from the busy world and, in the quietness of divine communion, discover the strength and fellowship of Your presence.

Portrait Thirteen
WHEN LIFE COMES TUMBLING DOWN

May the day of my birth perish (Job 3:3).

Job's trust in God had survived the calamitous loss of his property and posterity. Now the previous scene in heaven is repeated. Angels and Satan appear before God. The Lord commended Job, citing his integrity in spite of the ruination Satan brought on him. Satan scoffed, "But . . . strike his flesh and bones, and he will surely curse You." He implied that Job's own physical well-being was his most prized possession, and if God struck him there, Job's faith would fail.

Once again, God gave Satan a permission and a prohibition: "Very well, then, he is in your hands; but you must spare his life" (2:6).

Then the ultimate calamity fell on Job. Satan smote him with boils "from the soles of his feet to the top of his head." The descriptions of Job's suffering suggest it was a type of leprosy, perhaps elephantiasis, the most hideous, loathsome, painful disease known to the ancient world. His body covered with massive ulcerous sores, his limbs swollen, he became disfigured and unrecognizable (2:12). He was beset with intense itching, nightmares (7:14), and depression (7:16).

In his desolation, he sat among the ashes at the rubbish heap, with scavenger dogs and beggars outside the town, scraping himself with a potsherd. No doubt images of his ten precious children would flash on the screen of his tortured memory, along with flashbacks of his happy days of vigor and prestige. But now, like John Donne's succinct line of despair, "John Donne/Anne Donne/undone," so Job is "undone." Life had come tumbling down and was shattered.

Life can come tumbling down for any of us. A dream becomes shattered, a treasure is cruelly snatched from us, a loss rends the heart and leaves life bereft and desolate.

But God never allows us to suffer more than we can bear through His help. Ballington Booth's song reminds us of an assuring truth:

> The cross that He gave may be heavy,
>   But it ne'er outweighs His grace;
> The storm that I feared may surround me,
>   But it ne'er excludes His face.
>
> The cross is not greater than His grace,
>   The storm cannot hide His blessed face;
> I am satisfied to know, that with Jesus here below,
>   I can conquer every foe.
>
> The thorns in my path are not sharper
>   Than composed His crown for me;
> The cup which I drink not more bitter
>   Than He drank in Gethsemane.
>
> The light of His love shines the brighter
>   As it falls on paths of woe;
> The toil of my work will grow lighter
>   As I stoop to raise the low.

Lord, who stilled the turbulence of the raging Galilean Sea, when life's storms beat on us and the waves would engulf us, help us to hear Your word of power and peace.

Portrait Fourteen

THE CRISIS OF CHANGE -1-

Sighing comes to me instead of food (Job 3:24).

Job had gone through a crisis of change, a trauma of transition. He had gone from prosperity to poverty, from a happy family life to loneliness, from dignity and respect to the dunghill outside of town, from health to a horrible disease. In his lament of the third chapter, he groaned, "Sighing comes to me instead of food."

Dramatic and drastic change can be a crisis. We are comfortable with the familiar, there is security in the well-traveled path. Change requires adjustment, response, responsibility. Changes that challenge and test us come to each of our lives, sometimes to the limit of our resources and endurance.

An instructive study has been conducted by Dr. Thomas Holmes that measures the influence of change on our health. Dr. Holmes and his associates had discovered that disease often follows events of change, whether good or bad. From their research, they assigned points to common change-events with each point called a "life-change unit (LCU)." Dr. Holmes suggests that an accumulation of more than 200 of these units in one year could be the warning of a potential heart attack or health breakdown. Results showed that for those who scored over 300, there was an 80 percent chance for a major health change such as disease, surgery, accident, mental illness, etc. The following are examples from the Holmes Stress Chart giving rank, event, and LCU points.

RANK	EVENT	LCU POINTS
1	Death of spouse	100
2	Divorce	73
3	Marital separation	65
5	Death of a close family member	63
6	Personal injury or illness	53
7	Marriage	50
8	Fired at work	47
10	Retirement	45
11	Change in health of family member	44
12	Pregnancy	40
13	Sex difficulties	39
16	Change in financial state	38
17	Death of a close friend	37
18	Change to different line of work	36
23	Son or daughter leaving home	29
24	Trouble with in-laws	29
32	Change in residence	20
39	Change in number of family get-togethers	15
41	Vacation	13
42	Christmas	12

(Reprinted with permission of T.H. Holmes and R.H. Rahe. "The Social Adjustment Rating Scale," *Journal of Psychosomatic Research*, Pergamon Press, Copyright 1967, II:213.)

No doubt we could each add those events peculiar to our lives that also require adaptation and can cause stress. But, we follow the One who came to give us calm amid life's changes, peace amid its problems, triumph amid its turmoil, and conquest amid its conflicts.

> Eternal God, "Change and decay in all around I see; O Thou Who changest not, abide with me!" (Henry Francis Lyle)

Portrait Fifteen

THE CRISIS OF CHANGE -2-

Sighing comes to me instead of food (Job 3:24).

Many of us can remember when a village square was a place and not a person. "Setting the world on fire" was merely a figure of speech. A capsule traveled inside a man. Preachers were the only ones preparing people to travel to outer space. People were smarter than machines. A floppy disc was something you consulted a chiropractor about. Christmas trees were green and blackboards were black. As Bob Dylan sings, "The times, they are a changin'!"

For Job, the times changed radically. He found himself in a whole new world. He was transferred from a world of comfort and security to a world of crisis and desperation. It still happens. In a moment, life can change entirely.

One day Job was the richest man in the East; his sons were the strongest and his daughters the fairest in the land. The next day he was a pauper and alone. One day David married the king's daughter. The next the king hurled his javelin at him and chased him around the mountains as a wild animal. One day Daniel feasted at the king's table with 120 of the king's counselors. The next he was thrown in the lions' den.

Today we may march forth in health and vigor. But, suddenly, sickness unhinges our knees and we become horizontal citizens of the sickroom, unwilling initiates into the fellowship of pain. Misfortune can overtake us in a moment, shatter our dreams, and bring us to the brink of desperation.

Dramatic and dynamic change is the trademark of our time.

Alvin Toffler's popular book, *Future Shock*, was written to "help us survive our collision with tomorrow" as we are faced with "the death of permanence" and the accelerative thrust that brings us to the "limits of adaptability." It is written as a textbook with strategies for survival for those of us today who are overwhelmed by change and its hidden impacts.

But, of course, we already have a textbook for coping with the crisis of change. As we go on in the story of Job, we find that his faith and trust in God enabled him not only to survive, but to surmount the drastic changes that assaulted him. And, because we have the Paraclete, the Divine Presence called alongside to help us, we can affirm with songwriter Anna Waring:

> In heavenly love abiding,
>   No change my heart shall fear;
> And safe is such confiding,
>   For nothing changes here.
>
> The storm may roar without me,
>   My heart may low be laid;
> But God is round about me,
>   And can I be dismayed?
>
> Green pastures are before me
>   Which yet I have not seen;
> Bright skies will soon be o'er me,
>   Where the dark clouds have been.
>
> My hope I cannot measure,
>   My path to life is free;
> My Savior has my treasure,
>   And He will walk with me.

Father, amid the changes that surely will come, give me a steadfast faith and an abiding hope.

LIFE IS NOT FAIR

What I dreaded has happened to me (Job 3:25).

Job himself broke the silence with a soliloquy of despair. Edward Dhorme, eminent expositor of Job, describes this poem as "one of the most superb not only in the Bible but in the whole literature of the world."

Job's body was racked by relentless pain, his memory tortured with painful remembrance of the cherished joys of his children. His condition was so desperate that his wife suggested he curse God and kill himself.

His pent up torment erupted, and from the depths of his anguish, Job cried out against his suffering. No less than fourteen times, his anger exploded with a curse introduced by the word "may" (3:1-10). Fourteen times he hurled his anger at the heavens. Five times we also hear his protests with the word "why?" (3:11-23) However, his curses and protests were not against God but against his own contemptible existence.

He wished three things. First, that he had never been born (3:2-10): "May the day of my birth perish. . . . May it not be included among the days of the year." He wished his birthday could be erased from the calendar in history. Or, since he was born, he wished that he would have died at birth (3:11-19): "Why did I not perish at birth, and die as I came from the womb?"

But, having been born and surviving to this moment with his intolerable burden of sorrows and suffering, he wished he would die then, as he was among "those who long for death . . . who search for it more than for hidden treasure, who are filled with gladness and rejoice when they reach the grave." Job's poignant cry describes a man who has hit bottom and has nothing to live for: "What I feared has come upon me; what I dreaded has happened to me. I have no peace, no quietness; I have no rest but only turmoil" (3:25-26).

In his bestselling book, *When Bad Things Happen to Good People* (Avon), Rabbi Harold Kushner reminds us: "Life is not fair. The wrong people get sick and the wrong people get robbed and the wrong people get killed in wars and in accidents." As we journey further with Job in his trials and testings, we will see a classic example of bad things happening to good people.

The loss of our grandson, Jonathan, just at the time of his birth, brought this truth agonizingly home to us. Our daughter and her husband, with their beautiful spirit and commitment to the Lord, were undeserving of such a cruel loss. Indeed, life is not fair. But the Book of Job has a greater truth yet to reveal to us.

Sovereign God, let the dark threads of my life be interwoven with the tapestry of Your eternal purpose.

Portrait Seventeen
STRESS

I have no rest, but only turmoil (Job 3:26).

The third chapter of Job, known as Job's lament, is one of deep distress and despair. Job is under the greatest stress.

Trouble eventually knocks at everyone's door. Sometimes it doesn't bother to knock, but bangs the door down—ruthlessly, violently, unexpected, and unwanted.

Troubles will surely come. The plaintive warning of this book rings true across the centuries: "Man is born to trouble as surely as sparks fly up." Sometimes it is a far-off shadow, its approaching so slow as to be imperceptible. But, inexorably, it moves closer and will surely come to our door.

We will not only have our own problems. The problems of those we love and care for and for whom we have such high hopes and dreams hit us with full force as well. When tragedy strikes them, the quakes in their lives are registered on the Richter Scale of our own hearts.

So, what do we do when trouble bangs our door down? What do we do when we must journey alone into the dark cathedral of pain, into the dark places of sorrow, suffering, and ultimately, through the valley of death? Do we just give up, quit? Do we refuse to face reality? Do we become bitter against our fate? How do we cope with stress which surely comes to each life?

Biologist Hans Selye, considered the foremost authority on stress, defines it essentially as the wear and tear of living.

Books have been written on how to manage or avoid stress, for too often we may have found that stress manages us. We are all too well acquainted with its results of insomnia, headaches, elevated blood pressure, fatigue, irritation, muscle pain, tension, and inner turmoil. Chronic stress is suspected to be linked to heart disease and cancer.

Job's stresses are representative. He had financial stress. His wealth was wiped out in a matter of minutes. He had painful family stress with the loss of all his children and the despair of his wife. He knew status stress, being reduced from a renowned Edomite sheik to a disfigured pauper on the rubbish heap. He had health stress with the most hideous disease known at that time.

Perhaps each of us can identify with Job in some area of his stress. We are no strangers to discouragement and despair. So what do we do when we come to the end of our rope? Like Job, we tie a knot and hold on. We hold on by our faith in God and His enabling power. For we live in the era of the Holy Spirit, giving us a great plus that Job never knew. We not only can overcome, but God has promised we can be more than conquerors through Him who loved us (Rom. 8:37).

Fannie Jolliffe has given us a prayer song to help us confront life's dark and lonely days:

> I do not ask Thee, Lord,
>   That all my life may be
> An easy, smooth and pleasant path;
>   'Twould not be good for me.
>   But O I ask today
>   That grace and strength be given
> To keep me fighting all the way
>   That leads to God and heaven!
>
> I do not ask Thee, Lord,
>   That tears may never flow,
> Or that the world may always smile
>   Upon me as I go.
>   From Thee fell drops of blood;
>   A thorn-crown pressed Thy brow;

Thy suffering brought Thee victory then,
  And Thou canst help me now.

And what if strength should fail,
  And heart more deeply bleed?
Or what if dark and lonely days
  Draw forth the cry of need?
  That cry will bring Thee down
  My needy soul to fill,
And Thou wilt teach my yearning heart
  To know and do Thy will.

*Lord, who stilled the storm on turbulent Galilee, speak peace
to my heart; still any disquiet within; and make me adequate.*

Portrait Eighteen
BURNOUT

I have no peace, no quietness; I have no rest, but only turmoil (Job 3:26).

The hurried and harried pace of modern life has given us a new term for the syndrome of stress damage. *Burnout* is now the term commonly used to describe a state of mental, physical, and spiritual exhaustion brought on by continued stress. Job seems to be on the verge of burnout when he laments: "I have no peace, no quietness; I have no rest, but only turmoil (3:26).

Burnout is especially a danger to those involved in spiritual work and those who do "people work." It is a spiritual law that you cannot do work of a spiritual nature without energy going out from you. As you give yourself to others, you expend emotional, psychological, physical, and spiritual energy that make heavy drafts on your resources. Unless replenished, these resources will become depleted. There is the danger of giving out continually, without taking in, and ending up spiritually bankrupt. Burnout is the result of burning the candle at both ends. There is more heat and light for a time, but then it is consumed and the light and energy are gone.

Some of the great Christian leaders, who have been looked on as giants, have not been strangers to the dried-out condition. J.B. Phillips is well known for his striking and beautiful translation of the New Testament, as well as several popular books of Christian apologetics. But behind his renowned ministry was a constant struggle against depression. He put himself under the burden of great demands, confessing, "It seems I cannot get rid of colossal fantastic demands." His biographers write of him: "He knew anxiety and depression, from which there was only temporary release. For a period of fifty years, he had to cope with psychological disturbance and dark depression. . . . And while he never lost his faith in God, he never ceased to struggle against mental pain" (Vera Phillips and Edwin Robertson, *J.B. Phillips—The Wounded Healer*, Eerdmans, 1984, pg. viii, used by permission).

General William Booth, founder of The Salvation Army, came to a point of feeling drained and dried out more than once. Lonely and exhausted on an extensive traveling ministry, he wrote to his wife, Catherine: "I wonder if I could not get something to do in London of some kind, some secretaryship or something respectable that would keep us going" (Begbie, *The Life of General William Booth*, p. 422).

William Booth is remembered by Salvationists as a tower of strength, a man of unbounded energy, unrelenting in his warfare against sin. But here behind the scenes, we have a glimpse of his humanity and his being subject, as we all are, to depression in the face of exhaustion and hardship. However, it is the going on when life is difficult that makes a person great, that builds character, and enables that person to be used of God.

The Apostle Paul writes that he and his companions were "under great pressure, far beyond our ability to endure, so that we despaired even of life" (2 Cor. 1:8). Discouraged? Cheer up! You're in good company.

Herbert Booth has composed a song of faith for the difficult time, its last verse claiming a faith triumphant:

O for trust that brings the triumph
　　When defeat seems strangely near!
O for faith that changes fighting
　　Into victory's ringing cheer;
　　　Faith triumphant,
　　Knowing not defeat or fear!

Heavenly Father, when the outlook for my life is dim and dark, help me to take the uplook and see the light.

Portrait Nineteen
HOW NOT TO COMFORT

A word was secretly brought to me (Job 4:12).

We have been introduced to Job's comforters as they came on the scene in response to his calamities. At the shocking spectacle of Job in his sufferings, they broke forth in uncontrollable grief and then sat with him for seven days in stunned silence. They listened to Job's poignant lament and were ready to occupy center stage for most of the remainder of our story.

Eliphaz was the first to speak, his priority indicating he was the oldest. He commenced with a veiled apology and compliment. He recalled how Job has helped many in trouble and said, "Now trouble comes to you. . . . Should not your piety be your confidence?" (4:5-6) It was as though he was saying: "Physician, heal thyself."

Eliphaz wasted no time in hurling out his major and only premise—that Job's calamity was the result of sin: "Consider now: Who, being innocent, has ever perished? Where were the upright ever destroyed? As I have observed, those who plow evil and those who sow trouble reap it" (4:7-8).

"A word was secretly brought to me," said Eliphaz (4:12), as he claimed a vision from God. He vividly described a hair-raising experience: "the hair on my body stood on end" (4:15). After all, who can debate the authority of someone who says, "God has spoken to me." It leaves no room for discussion. Thus Eliphaz spoke with absolute dogmatism.

He rubbed salt into Job's wounds by suggesting his sin had caused the loss of his children (5:3-4). Job's afflictions were attributed to the corrections of God, and he was advised to "not despise the discipline of the Almighty" (5:17).

Eliphaz broke all the rules of offering counsel and comfort. From him we can learn the negatives to avoid when people are hurting. His arrogance instructs us not to be dogmatic, judgmental, insensitive, theologically naive, and superficial. Often, people in trouble do not need our words and our philosophies; they need us. They need our love, our caring, our compassion, our affirmation, our practical support, and encouragement.

The late General Albert Orsborne, in one of his songs, reminds us of the priority of compassion in our being used of God for others:

It is not with might to establish the right,
  Nor yet with the wise to give rest;
The mind cannot show what the heart longs to know
  Nor comfort a people distressed.
O Savior of men, touch my spirit again,
  And grant that Thy servant may be
Intense every day, as I labor and pray,
  Both instant and constant for Thee.

Except I am moved with compassion,
  How dwelleth Thy spirit in me?
    In word and in deed
    Burning love is my need;
  I know I can find this in Thee.

Loving Father, give to me a compassion that will enable me to be a comfort and strength to those who are hurting and distressed.

Portrait Twenty
BORN TO TROUBLE

*Man is born to trouble as surely as sparks fly upward
(Job 5:7).*

God never promised us a Disneyland.

Some of the most profound truths and stately statements in the Book of Job come from the lips of his contestants. Though Job's friends were flawed in their theology, the universal truths that they uttered merit our consideration. One such timeless truth came from Eliphaz: "Man is born to trouble as surely as sparks fly upward."

As universal as this truth is, many do not accept it or are not prepared to live by it. "Life is difficult," writes Dr. Scott Peck. He goes on to state: "This is a great truth, one of the greatest truths. . . . Most do not fully see this truth that life is difficult. Instead, they moan more or less incessantly, noisily or subtly, about the enormity of their problems, their burdens, and their difficulties as if life were generally easy, as if life should be easy. . . . Life is a series of problems" (*The Road Less Traveled*, Simon & Schuster, 1978, p. 15).

This fundamental truth elucidated by Dr. Peck in his integration of the insights of psychiatry and his faith is only an amplification of the Book of Job. It was clearly and bluntly stated centuries before in this simple statement: "Man is born to trouble." It is one of the most universal of all truths. To live successfully, we must accept this truth and be prepared to cope with its meaning.

It is an obvious lesson of Christian history that believers

have not been immune from suffering and the consequences of living in a depraved world. The disciples of our Lord were called to a cross and, in the end, they paid the ultimate price of discipleship. Andrew was bound to a cross. Bartholomew was flayed alive. James the Greater was beheaded and James the Less was stoned to death. Jude met a violent death. Matthew was slain by the sword. Peter was crucified. Philip was hanged. Simon was crucified. Thomas was pierced with a lance.

The Apostle Paul three times took a course on "How to survive shipwreck." Another lesson he mastered was "How to escape when held hostage" as he was let down over the city wall in a basket. In his catalog of sufferings, he refers to stonings, floggings, imprisonments, and other trials that would have turned back any but the totally committed. Still, Paul was able to testify, "I have learned to be content whatever the circumstances" (Phil. 4:11). In the end, he was beheaded in Rome. Discipleship was a very costly business in those days.

Helen Hayes and her husband lost their nineteen-year-old daughter to polio. Her husband never quit asking, "Why should it happen to us? We never hurt anybody. Why? Why? Why?" Helen Hayes, seeing the suffering of other people, replied, "Why not us?"

As the Book of Job reminds us, trouble is the common lot of our humanity. We are not without resources that will enable us to cope.

Christ of the Gethsemane Garden, help me in my hour of trial to find in prayer the strength to go on.

A LITERARY MASTERPIECE

He performs wonders that cannot be fathomed, miracles that cannot be counted (Job 5:9).

The writer of Job is the Shakespeare of the Bible. The Book of Job is considered a classic within and outside of religious circles. It has universal appeal, a timeless theme, memorable language, and a message for the ages.

The Book of Job has been extolled for its literary excellence, more than any other book of the Bible. Victor Hugo extravagantly asserts, "The Book of Job is perhaps the greatest masterpiece of the human mind." Thomas Carlyle eulogizes, "There is nothing written, I think . . . of equal literary merit." Luther is equally immoderate, praising it as "magnificent and sublime as no other book of Scripture." Philip Schaff adds the accolade: "The Book of Job rises like a pyramid in the history of literature, without a predecessor and without a rival." J.A. Froude sets it "towering far above all the poetry of the world." Alfred Tennyson lauds it as "the greatest poem of ancient or modern times."

"The literary mastery of the poet is unsurpassed," acclaims Samuel Terrien. David L. McKenna adds a contemporary credit: "From a literary standpoint, Job is a monumental book—one of a kind. . . . Where can you find such passionate poetry, dialectical prose, soaring allegory, majestic songs and quotable quotes?"

The sandwich literary structure of Job consists of three

parts: prose prologue (1–2), poetic dialogue (3:1–42:26), and prose epilogue (42:7-17). This literary structure and the theological insights are creatively interwoven into a devotional tapestry of timeless truths.

How marvelous are the ways of God. From the deepest depths of despair recorded in the Bible, He brings out the loftiest literature of the ages. Out of calamity, He gives the world this celebrated classic. With Job we exclaim, "He performs wonders that cannot be fathomed, miracles that cannot be counted."

The lofty literary quality of this book eloquently proclaims that we have a God who can bring triumph out of trial and blessing out of the brokenness of our lives.

Eternal God, as I explore the riches and beauty of this book, with the psalmist I pray, "Open my eyes that I may see wonderful things in Your Law" (Ps. 119:18).

THE SUPREME SUFFERER

If only my anguish could be weighed. . . . It would surely
outweigh the sand of the seas (Job 6:1-2).

In response to the insensitive torrent of Eliphaz's words, Job
cried out:

> If only my anguish could be weighed
> and all my misery placed on the scales!
> It would surely outweigh the sand of the seas.

There are still those who feel the crushing weight of sorrow
and trial. No doubt all of us have known someone who has
gone through a tragedy that seemed impossible to endure. As
I write this paragraph, we have learned of a beautiful young
Christian couple tortured and murdered just this week before
Christmas, an act of horrible and wanton brutality in our
world of violence. For their loved ones, Job's words express
their being overwhelmed with sorrow.

But when we read the Book of Job, we also need to keep in
mind the New Testament. For there we find hope and
strength. There we also find an incredible fact. We discover
that God Himself became the supreme Sufferer on our behalf.

Some notable men are men of wealth, some are men of
fame, some are men of pleasure, but Christ was a Man of
Sorrows. He was the God who became "pierced for our trans-
gressions . . . crushed for our iniquities . . . and by His wounds

we are healed" (Isa. 53:5). There is no pain He has not felt, no sorrow He has not borne, no suffering He has not endured, no loneliness He has not known. And it was all for us. Such divine love is too deep for us to plumb its majesty and mystery.

Joni Eareckson Tada, whose writings and story have become such an inspiration, felt her whole world collapse when she became a quadriplegic from a diving accident at the age of seventeen. She found her condition impossible to reconcile with a loving God. Following her accident she went through three years of bitterness and questioning.

One night, Cindy, one of Joni's closest friends, was beside her bed trying to help Joni come out of her despair. She suddenly blurted out, "Joni, Jesus knows how you feel—you aren't the only one—why, He was paralyzed too." Joni glared at her. "What? What are you talking about?" Cindy continued, "It's true. Remember, He was nailed on a cross. His back was raw from beatings, and He must have yearned for a way to move to change positions, or redistribute His weight. But He couldn't. He was paralyzed by the nails, unable to move."

It was a moment of revelation for Joni. She writes: "God became incredibly close to me. . . . I guess every Christian with an experience similar to mine goes back to the Book of Job for answers. Here was a righteous man who suffered more than I could imagine. Everything was taken away from him. Strangely, the Book of Job does not answer any questions about why God let the tragedies happen. But Job clung to God. . . . Maybe God's gift to me is my dependence on Him."

And that's something of what this Book of Job is all about.

Lord, help me not to seek comfort in place of the cross, security in place of sacrifice, but enable me to take up my cross and follow in Your path.

THE DEVOTION OF FRIENDS -1-

A despairing man should have the devotion of his friends (Job 6:14).

Helen Parker in her poem reminds us of life's greatest discovery:

Today a man discovered gold and fame;
Another flew the stormy seas;
Another saw an unnamed world aflame;
One found the germ of a disease.
But what high fates my paths attend:
For I—today I found a friend!

No one of us is an island. We need the friendship, support, affirmation, and encouragement of others. When we confront trials and ultimate tests, then loved ones and friends will be sources of comfort and strength that will make a difference. Sometimes it will not be by their words but by their caring and presence.

Henry Ford changed the economic life of our country in his production of cars and employment practice. He was the first employer in American history to pay a wage of five dollars a day. One day, when a young man came to visit him, the great industrialist looked him in the eye and then took a piece of paper and wrote the question: "Who is your best friend?" Ford himself then answered it: "Your best friend is he or she who helps you bring out of yourself the best that is in you."

Job's friends, in their visit and attempt to comfort him, though much of their approach was misdirected, brought the best out of Job. Their challenge to him brought out his greatness; their imputations reinforced his faith; their flawed theology required Job to crystallize and reaffirm his own faith.

True friendship has its rigorous demands. It requires the gift of time, of honesty, of a vulnerable involvement for the good of the other. These are beyond the price some are willing to pay and, consequently, they forfeit life's great gift of friendships. Anyone who has been graced with true friendship knows its cost and its worth.

All humanity identifies with Job's deep longing: "A despairing man should have the devotion of his friends." When we are hurting, nothing is as comforting as a good friend.

Heavenly Father, thank You for loved ones and friends who have been an encouragement and inspiration to go on when life has been difficult.

THE DEVOTION OF FRIENDS -2-

A despairing man should have the devotion of his friends (Job 6:14).

When sorrow and tragedy strike, and we are tempted to ask, "Where is God? Why does He not come to me?"—let us remember Browning's insight: "Hush, I pray you! What if this friend happens to be God?"

If God at times draws near us through the beauty and wonder of nature, how much more can He draw near through our friends? If He speaks to us through the tones of the wind and the murmuring of the sea, how much clearer can He speak to us through the vibrant voices of our friends?

Sadly, instead of Job's friends being comforters to him, they were contestants. Instead of alleviation, they were an aggravation. Instead of diminishing his woes, they deepened them. With vivid imagery and satire, he lamented that his "friends" are as desert streams that have become bone-dry when parched travelers come expecting to quench their thirsts (6:14-20).

One of the great Greek words of the New Testament is *koinonia*, translated "fellowship." It is a word rich with meaning, used to express the most intimate kinds of human relationship. But it is more than a word. It is one of the richest heritages and experiences of the Christian. It is a special gift of God to the believer.

We read of the Christians in the New Testament church that "They devoted themselves to . . . fellowship" (Acts 2:42).

They did not merely have fellowship; they "devoted" themselves to it. For those early Christians, it was not a luxury; it was a necessity. It was not merely a social activity; it was a spiritual communion. It was a bond, a union in Christ. It was a sharing together in joint partnership, a communion of believers. The early church was a severely persecuted church; it was a suffering church. They needed each other and were sustained by the supportive and affirming fellowship.

Thomas Kelly writes of this fellowship: "In glad amazement and wonder we enter upon a relationship which we had not known the world contained for the sons of men. Why should such bounty be given to unworthy men like ourselves?" Thank God for such enriching and sustaining fellowship and for the devotion of our friends when we may be despairing.

With John Fawcett, we join in song:

> Blest be the tie that binds
>   Our hearts in Christian love;
> The fellowship of kindred minds
>   Is like to that above.
>
> Before our Father's throne
>   We pour our ardent prayers;
> Our fears, our hopes, our aims are one,
>   Our comforts and our cares.
>
> We share our mutual woes,
>   Our mutual burdens bear;
> And often for each other flows
>   The sympathizing tear.

Father in heaven, may I ever be grateful for the devotion of my friends and may I be a faithful friend to others in their times of need.

Portrait Twenty-five
WHAT JOB DID NOT LOSE

My integrity is at stake (Job 6:29).

Job is the story of a man who lost everything.

We remember his calamitous losses—his possessions, his family, his health, and finally, the respect of his peers. Yes, Job was the man who lost everything.

But to remember Job that way is to miss the whole point of his story. For Job did not lose everything. He held onto that which is most precious—that which the most severe loss and suffering, and even death, cannot destroy or take from us. For the story of Job is the story of a man who kept his faith in spite of the worst misfortunes, in spite of his world tumbling down around him, in spite of crushing heartbreak.

It is one man's story, but it is every man's story. Each of us may be called on to hold onto his faith in the midst of severe testings and trials.

J.B., the play by Archibald MacLeish, brings the drama of Job up to date with the story of a man and wife who suffered the loss of their five children to war, an auto accident, and crime. Many life stories in modern context echo the testing of faith through trial and tragedy.

Who of us would claim to be exempt from the strategies and subtleties of Satan; from the testings and temptations, and perhaps the tragedies, that try men's souls? Who of us, with Job, is not constrained to say in the contests of life, "My integrity is at stake"?

Sooner or later, we each come to our Jobian crossroads. When we do, we all ask the same questions: "Why?" "Where is God?" "Why do bad things happen to good people?" "And good things to bad people?" "Is pain without purpose?" "How can I be adequate?" "How can I maintain my faith and not go under?"

From Job's story comes God's message to us, that when testing and tragedy come, our trust in God can see us through. It assures us with the central message that when we cannot understand the "why" of life, we can still know the "who," and that will make the difference.

The Book of Job will not give ready answers to the mystery of suffering and the cosmic issue of pain. But it gives a perspective and reveals the triumph of faith in the crucible of suffering.

> *Eternal God, as I commence my journey through this great book You have given us, may the Holy Spirit, the Revealer of truth, illumine my mind and open my heart to its radiant revelations and timeless truths.*

THE BREVITY OF LIFE

My days are swifter than a weaver's shuttle (Job 7:6).

The brevity of life is especially impressed on us in times of crisis and life-threatening situations. Job, reflecting while sitting on his dung heap, felt that the good part of his life was behind him. It had all gone by so quickly. The pathos of his words echo down through the centuries: "My days are swifter than a weaver's shuttle." Later he exclaimed:

Man born of woman is of few days and full of trouble.
He springs up like a flower and withers away;
like a fleeting shadow, he does not endure (14:1-2).

And on another occasion, he reiterated the same theme:

Only a few years will pass
before I go on the journey of no return (16:22).

Job would remind all of us how brief our lives are. With Andrew Marvell, we sense the remorseless rush of time: "But at my back I always hear/Time's wingèd chariot hurrying near." Shakespeare expressed this transience in memorable words:

Life's but a walking shadow
A poor player

That struts and frets
　His hour upon the stage
And then is heard no more.

Time indeed steals our years and life away. It will write wrinkles on our faces, scribble crow's feet about our eyes, and paint our hair white. It is the one preacher to whom all must listen. Professor Time, that venerable pedagogue, teaches his lessons well.

Thornton Wilder's play, *Our Town*, is pregnant with spiritual meaning. Emily, the main character, dies giving birth to a child. In the afterlife, she is granted her one wish, that of watching herself and her family live out one day of the life she left behind. She chooses her twelfth birthday. As an invisible observer, she is dismayed at how her family does not realize how precious life is and how important they are to each other. She agonizes over their wasting infinitely precious time. Turning to the audience in the play, she asks: "Do any human beings ever realize life while they live it?"

Job's plaintive reflections on life's brevity serve notice to take life seriously. We are to invest, not waste, the precious deposit into each day's account of 86,400 seconds, 1,440 minutes, 24 hours. We must spend them all that same day. None can be carried over the next day. As someone has said, "Life is a coin. You can spend it any way you want to, but you can only spend it once."

With the psalmist let us affirm: "My times are in your hands" (Ps. 31:15). Then we can make each twenty-four shining hours a stairway to the stars, an investment for eternity.

Eternal God, help me to so pass through things temporal that I shall not lose that which is eternal.

Portrait Twenty-seven
THE FORMER GENERATIONS

> *Ask the former generations and find out what their fathers learned (Job 8:8).*

Bildad now took up where Eliphaz left off. He was an exponent of tradition and he urged:

> Ask the former generations and find out
>   what their fathers learned,
> for we were born only yesterday and know nothing,
> and our days on earth are but a shadow.
> Will they not instruct you and tell you?
> Will they not bring forth words from their
> understanding? (8:8-10)

There is, of course, wisdom in the counsel that Bildad offered Job. We need to tap the rich reservoir of the past, the legacy of thought and experience that has gone on before. We are immeasurably enriched by the former generations who kept the faith and triumphed in their trials and testings. Longfellow expressed it in unforgettable lines in his "Psalm of Life":

> Lives of great men all remind us
>   We too can make our lives sublime
> And departing leave behind us
>   Footprints in the sands of time;

Footprints, that perhaps another,
  Sailing o'er life's solemn main,
A forlorn and shipwrecked brother,
  Seeing, shall take heart again.

We are all heavy debtors to former generations. I readily acknowledge my incalculable debt to generations of writers who have been sources of precious and priceless inspiration. The centuries instruct the years, and we would do well to heed Bildad's advice to let them "bring forth words from their understanding" (8:10).

Tradition holds not only profit but peril. It can freeze progress. Its epitaph reads, "We have never done it this way." It can lock us into a flawed philosophy or theology.

This was the problem with Bildad's call on the ancients. All he and his companions had to offer Job in his suffering were the outmoded aphorisms of tradition. Theirs was the lock-step tradition that suffering is always caused by sin, as Bildad pontificated: "Surely God does not reject a blameless man or strengthen the hands of evildoers" (8:20). This flawed theology was prevalent in the Eastern religions of that day that believed God rewards the righteous and punishes the unrighteous. Thus, they reasoned, Job's suffering was the consequence of his sin.

Our text cautions that we should take care in the sources we consult and cite. Let us be discerning in taking the true and best from tradition and rejecting the false and misleading. Often a false religion or a cult will have seized on some valid point that seems to give credibility to its cause. Even a clock that is stopped is right twice a day. But we do not plan or pursue our lives by it.

Heavenly Father, help me to discerningly tap the legacy of thought and experience of great hearts of yesteryear. Thank You for the contribution they have made and will make to my life.

THE DIVINE POTTER

> *Your hands shaped me and made me. . . . You molded me like clay (Job 10:8-9).*

"I loathe my very life" (10:1) was the pathetic cry of Job in reply to Bildad, with these two chapters, 9 and 10, representing the nadir of Job's experience. To Bildad's insensitive assertions, Job replied with great pathos: "Turn away from me so I can have a moment's joy before I go to the place of no return, to the land of gloom and deep shadow" (10:20-21).

Yet, even in the depths of his despair, he included a doxology on the wonders of God (9:4-10), exclaiming:

> His wisdom is profound, His power is vast. . . .
> He performs wonders that cannot be fathomed,
>   miracles that cannot be numbered.

Though in torment, Job did not lose sight of the majesty and sovereignty of God. This insight and assurance sustained him and was always as a light for him in his otherwise deep darkness.

A.W. Tozer has written, "No man's religion ever rises higher than his concept of God." Job had a proper concept of the greatness of God. Let us beware lest our God be too small and we lose the assurance of His sovereignty.

Job affirmed that humanity is God's special creation (10:8-12), likening Him to the potter who skillfully molds and fashions his work:

Your hands shaped me and made me. . . .
Remember that You molded me like clay. . . .
You gave me life and showed me kindness.

Job's metaphor of God as the Potter and we as the clay is a good one for us to remember. If we yield our lives to Him, He will fashion it into a vessel of beauty and purpose. Leslie Taylor-Hunt has expressed this thought in a song of prayer:

Now is my will resigned,
  Struggles are quelled;
Clay on the wheel am I,
  Nothing withhold.
Master, I yield to Thee,
Crumble, then fashion me
Flawless, and fit to be
  Indwelt by Thee.

The paradox of the Christian life is that in surrender we find victory, in our yielding we are made strong, in rendering up our sword to Him we become conquerors.

Divine Potter, mold and make me after Your will, fashion me in the likeness of Christ my Lord. Then shall I be a vessel fit for the Master's use.

Portrait Twenty-nine

THE LIMITS OF THE ALMIGHTY

Can you probe the limits of the Almighty? (Job 11:7)

In one of the loftiest passages of the book, Zophar affirmed the wisdom of God and declared His absolute knowledge of men. He asked Job the rhetorical question:

Can you fathom the mysteries of God?
Can you probe the limits of the Almighty? (11:7)

In our day of casual religious culture, we need to recapture the sense of the transcendence of God. Indeed, as Zophar stated, the mysteries and limits of God "are higher than the heavens" (11:8). There is a mystery and majesty of God that transcends our most daring imaginings. We have only received but a glimpse of His glory, a whisper of His wonder. We who are but creatures of a day cannot begin to fathom the eternal God.

We would not want it otherwise. For if my finite mind could grasp the infinite, then the infinite would be finite. We want a God greater than our understanding, a God beyond the probe of our minds and satellites, a God higher than the utmost reach of man's ultimate questings. The Book of Job reminds us that we have just such a God.

Let us come before Him in praise and adoration. In the words of Albert Dalziel's song, let us exalt and praise our sovereign God:

Eternal God, unchanging
    Through all the changing years,
Whose hands all things created,
    Who holds the countless stars;
Enthroned in heavenly glory,
    Yet not a God afar;
Thou deignest to have dwelling
    Here where Thy people are.

Though men have wrought confusion
    Thy hand still holds the plan.
And Thou, at length, decideth
    The destiny of man;
Dominions rise and perish,
    The mighty have their day,
But still Thy Word abideth,
    It shall not pass away.

Sovereign God, who holds the stars and galaxies on their un-erring courses, thank You for holding my frail and finite life in Your mighty hands.

Portrait Thirty
PIETY AND PROSPERITY

> *If you devote your heart to Him . . . you will surely forget your trouble (Job 11:13-16).*

"Are all these words to go unanswered?" (11:2) asked Zophar as he took over the discussion. With greater bluntness and rudeness than the others, he challenged: "Will no one rebuke you when you mock?" (11:3) Zophar was the least sparing of all, calling Job a phony, in essence saying, "You're not the 'Mr. Clean' you claim to be."

He followed the same reasoning as Eliphaz and Bildad, urging Job to repent of his sin. The orations of the three contestants were based on the flawed theology that virtue brings fortune and sin brings misfortune. It had a kinship in that day with the Eastern religions. Their syllogism of deterministic theology was: Suffering is punishment for sin; Job is suffering greatly; therefore, Job has sinned greatly.

In other words, it pays to be religious. Piety is wedded to prosperity. The most vigorous assertion of the three was that God makes good men prosper and evil men suffer.

Prosperity theology is a religious phenomenon of our day. We hear that Christians are to enjoy substantial wealth and continued health, and are told in a variety of ways how to attain prosperity and success through our faith. Modern culture has negated the punch line of the old story of the pulpit committee that prayed, "Lord, just send us a poor, humble preacher to lead us. That's all we ask. In fact, we'll even help—You keep him humble, and we'll keep him poor!"

Charles Colson warns us of this danger: "Success is all that counts. . . . That secular mentality has insidiously infiltrated and influenced our theology. Much of today's teaching and preaching communicates Christianity as an instant fix to all our pains and struggles. Consequently, we begin to think of our faith as a sparkling magic wand; we wave it, and presto, our problems are gone in a puff of smoke. But this is, bluntly put, pure heresy" (*Who Speaks for God?* Crossway Books, 1985, p. 31).

Job's three friends were well versed in their theology. In the New Testament, our Lord makes it crystal clear that He calls us not to self-indulgence but to self-denial, not to a frolic but to a fight, not to a picnic but to a pilgrimage, not to security but to sacrifice, not to comfort but to a cross.

Amy Carmichael had no illusions about the cost of discipleship. She served as a missionary in India for over fifty years without a return to her homeland. While bedridden some twenty years before her death, she wrote:

From prayer that asks that I may be
Sheltered from winds that beat on Thee,
From fearing when I should aspire,
From faltering when I should climb higher,
From silken self, O Captain, free
Thy soldier who would follow Thee.

From subtle love of softening things,
From easy choices, weakenings,
(Not thus are spirits fortified,
Not this way went the Crucified)
From all that dims Thy Calvary,
O Lamb of God, deliver me.

Give me the love that leads the way,
The faith that nothing can dismay,
The hope no disappointments tire,
The passion that will burn like fire,
Let me not sink to be a clod:
Make me Thy fuel, Flame of God.

Portrait Thirty-one

THERAPY OF HUMOR

Doubtless . . . wisdom will die with you! (Job 12:2)

To their pious claim of superior knowledge of God's ways with man, Job retorted: "Doubtless you are the people and wisdom will die with you!" (12:2) Andrew Blackwood calls this "the most humorous verse in the entire Bible."

With this chapter, the momentum changes. It was then a new Job who spoke as he took the offensive. For the first time, he reacted with sarcasm to their harsh judgments.

Job labeled their arguments as commonplace and trivial: "Who does not know all these things?" (12:3) In this three-chapter rebuttal, he called his contestants "quacks": "You are worthless physicians, all of you!" (13:4) And like the speaker of whom it was said, "He could not have said less unless he had said more," Job satirized: "If only you would be altogether silent! For you, that would be wisdom" (13:5).

Job may have lost his possessions, but he did not lose his sense of humor. To be able to see the humorous side of a situation redeems many an otherwise hopeless predicament. Norman Cousins has written in *The Anatomy of an Illness* (Norton, 1979): "I was greatly elated by the discovery that there is a physiological basis for the ancient theory that laughter is good medicine." And psychiatrist William Fry believes that virtually all body systems are influenced by humor.

The writer of Proverbs expressed this truth centuries earlier: "A cheerful heart is a good medicine" (Prov. 17:22). The preacher in Ecclesiastes would remind us that there is "a time to laugh" (Ecc. 3:4). Learning to see the humorous side of things is one of the most serious subjects in the world to master. When life loses its humor, it is hard to be spiritual. Thomas Merton wrote, "The mark of a saint is the ability to laugh."

When Victor Frankl was in a German concentration camp, he made a pact with another prisoner. Every day they would tell each other a funny story. Every day they would find a joke in their experience in that hell that was Auschwitz. Incredible as it may seem, they were able to do that, and it helped keep them sane and able to survive.

How instructive it is to note that the Book of Job, the saddest story of the Bible, has some of the most humorous verses of the Bible. When we come near the end of this book, we will see an example of God's humor as He chides Job.

Are you going through a difficult experience? Stand back for a moment and capture a perspective that will enable you to laugh through your tears and trials. Humor and laughter are great gifts of God and can be a therapy in time of trouble.

Lord, help me not to lose my sense of humor, no matter how difficult life may become. Help me to know the tonic of laughter and the therapy of seeing the comical in life's twists and turns.

Portrait Thirty-two
WHEN OTHERS SLIP
AND FALL

Men at ease have contempt for misfortune as the fate of those whose feet are slipping (Job 12:5).

A sad truth fell from the lips of Job: "Men at ease have contempt for misfortune as the fate of those whose feet are slipping" (12:5). How often have believers put on their "gossip list" instead of on their prayer list those who have fallen! David L. McKenna gives a painful description of this fault: "A certain ghoulish glee always attends the downfall of the high and the migthy. Jealous tongues cluck with juicy gossip whenever a great person shows signs of weakness, makes a false move, or experiences a failure. Americans in particular cannot countenance human weakness in their leaders. The slightest physical flaw in a President sends the stock market spinning downward and starts the cartoonists' pencils doodling caricatures that make the person a laughingstock" (David L. McKenna, *The Communicator's Commentary—Job*, Word Books, 1986).

Job, once the most respected and renowned man of his day, lamented, "I have become a laughingstock to my friends" (12:4). Someone of our day has made the caustic comment: "Christians are the only ones who shoot their wounded." A lesson we can learn from the Book of Job is how to respond to those who suffer or fall.

People around us are hurting. There are those whose feet have slipped on the pathway of the cross. They do not need others to stand back to criticize and condemn. They need us to stretch out a helping hand, to uplift, to be friends in need. Let us be encouragers on the road of life, and our prayer be that of Charles Wesley:

> Help us to help each other, Lord,
>   Each other's cross to bear;
> Let each his friendly aid afford,
>   And feel his brother's care.
>
> Help us to build each other up,
>   Our little stock improve;
> Increase our faith, confirm our hope,
>   And perfect us in love.

Dear Lord, lead me today to pray for a comrade who is hurting, to speak the word of encouragement to the one whose feet have slipped on the pathway of the cross.

THE WEAPON OF TRUTH

The tents of marauders are undisturbed (Job 12:6).

Job now made a frontal attack on the deterministic theology of his contestants. He depicted by example the absurdity of their reasoning that equated virtue with fortune and sin with misfortune: "The tents of marauders are undisturbed, and those who provoke God are secure" (12:6). He cited the obvious fact that the wicked often prosper and dwell in peace and security. The facts of life do not fit their theories.

And, not only do the wicked prosper, but the righteous will suffer, for trouble is the common lot of man: "Man born of woman is of few days and full of trouble" (14:1). This is one of the most profound truths of life with which we must come to terms.

Job the realist had dealt a stunning blow to the specious theory of a prosperity religion. These lock-step traditionalists have been challenged by the light of truth and reality. They will never fully recover from it, for as James Russell Lowell would remind us in "The Present Crisis":

> Truth forever on the scaffold,
>   Wrong forever on the throne—
> Yet that scaffold sways the future,
>   and, behind the dim unknown,
> Standeth God within the shadow,
>   keeping watch above His own.

In this drama of Job's great test and tragedy, he steadfastly maintained his faith in God and the reality of His truth and ways with man. In the end, that will make the difference.

God is sovereign. Ultimately, evil will be vanquished and righteousness shall reign.

Heavenly Father, give me a clear perspective on the reality of my life and world and help me to ever be assured that You are Ruler yet.

Portrait Thirty-four
ALL NATURE SPEAKS

But ask the animals, and they will teach you (Job 12:7).

In Job's rebuttal to Zophar, he told him to look to nature and it will teach him of God. He cited three categories of fauna and the earth itself as a source of instruction about God (12:7-9).

First, "But ask the animals, and they will teach you." Ask a chipmunk with a body barely six inches long who made it able to carry and hide more than a bushel of acorns in just three days so he will be prepared for the long winter. Ask the snowshoe hare who turns its fur white only in the winter and the fawn who gave it spots to camouflage it from predators. Ask the sleek cheetah, the fastest land animal, who made it able to reach speeds of seventy miles an hour. Let the animals teach us of the marvelous endowments and providence of their Creator.

Job went on: "Ask . . . the birds of the air, and they will tell you." Ask millions of birds who endowed them with the marvel of migration as their feathered power takes them incredible distances, with the champion migrant—the small arctic tern—making an annual round trip of over 20,000 miles. Ask the ruby-throated hummingbird, weighing only an eighth of an ounce, who made it able to fly 500 miles across the Gulf of Mexico, its wings beating fifty times a second. Ask the birds and they will tell you who teaches them their solar and stellar navigation, who planted their inbuilt compasses enabling them to span continents and oceans. And ask the brown bat who enables it to emit sounds at 90,000 vibrations per second and, listening to the echo, to hunt and find its food on the wing. Far more than Job ever knew in his day, the birds are able to tell us about the marvels of God's creative handiwork.

"Or speak to the earth," Job went on, "and it will teach you." What eloquence is spoken by creation in the miracle of seedtime and harvest, of the tapestry of a tree, the exquisite beauty of a flower, the spectacle of a sunrise that causes all the earth to blush at the extravagant beauty it is about to unveil.

"Or let the fish of the sea inform you," added Job. The infinite variety, the incredible fecundity, and the exotic creations of marine life testify to a God of unlimited imagination and creativity.

Annie Dillard, in her delightful book, *Pilgrim at Tinker Creek*, writes, "The extravagant gesture is the very stuff of creation. . . . The whole show has been on fire from the word go. . . . Not only did the Creator create everything, but He is apt to create anything. He'll stop at nothing. . . . The Creator loves pizzazz" (Harper & Row, pp. 9, 135, 137).

Job would heartily agree with the affirmation of Maltbie Babcock's popular song in our hymnbooks (Scribners):

This is my Father's world,
    And to my listening ears,
All nature sings and round me rings
    The music of the spheres.
This is my Father's world,
    I rest me in the thought
Of rocks and trees, of skies and seas;
    His hand the wonders wrought.

Heavenly Father, keep me open and aware to the wonder and beauty of Your creation. Save me from ever becoming blasé before such beauty or dull to its wonders.

Portrait Thirty-five

JOB'S VOW

Though He slay me, yet will I hope in Him (Job 13:15).

In Job's fourth speech, we find one of the most sublime statements in the Old Testament, in spite of its difficulty of translation. From the depths of his torment and tragedy, Job vowed: "Though He slay me, yet will I hope in Him" (13:15).

This vow has all the greater meaning because of the night-enshrouded setting in which it was uttered.

Job seemingly had lost everything. Even his wife told him to "curse God and die." And now, in the final trial of his friends assailing his integrity and impeaching him with their invectives, Job maintained his trust in God, even if God should slay him. It is one of the high points of trust recorded in the Bible and annals of human history.

From his ash dung heap hostel, Job uttered a testimony that can keep believers triumphant amid the worst that life can throw at them. Joni Eareckson Tada eloquently and remarkably illustrates this truth in testifying: "My paralysis has drawn me close to God and given a spiritual healing which I wouldn't trade for a hundred active years on my feet." When everything else in life may be shattered, we can still hold on to that which is most precious—God Himself. Our trust in Him is not subject to the trials and vicissitudes of life.

May we with Job, with Joni, and with Ella Wheeler Wilcox ("I Will Not Doubt," Harper & Row) have an unflinching faith that says:

I will not doubt, though all my ships at sea
Come drifting home with broken masts and sails;
I shall believe the hand that never fails,
From seeming evil worketh good for me.
And though I weep because those sails are battered,
Still will I cry, while my best hopes are shattered,
   I trust in Thee.

I will not doubt, though sorrows fall like rain,
And troubles swarm like bees about a hive;
I shall believe the heights for which I strive
Are only reached by anguish and by pain;
And though I groan and tremble with my crosses,
I yet shall see, through my severest losses,
   The greatest gain.

I will not doubt, well anchored in the faith,
Like some staunch ship, my soul braves every gale,
So strong its courage that it will not fail,
To breast the mighty unknown sea of death;
Oh, may I cry, when body parts with spirit,
I do not doubt, so listening worlds may hear it.

*Lord, increase my faith to withstand the storms, so when they
beat on my frail bark on the sea of life, I shall be able to say, "I
trust in You."*

Portrait Thirty-six

OF FEW DAYS AND FULL OF TROUBLE

> *Man born of woman is of few days and full of trouble (Job 14:1).*

When life flows along smoothly we are not so conscious of the frailty and brevity of life. But when crisis or a life-threatening situation comes on us, we suddenly come face-to-face with the vulnerability of life. Job's desperate plight constrained him to confess:

> Man born of woman
> is of few days and full of trouble.
> He springs up like a flower and withers away;
> like a fleeting shadow, he does not endure (14:1-2).

Life at its longest is still as a quickly withering flower or a fleeting shadow. The older one becomes, the more awareness is there of this truth. No one in their mature years can look back without a sense of life having flown by. Poignantly, one asks: "Where has it all gone? How could it have gone by so quickly?"

There is a pathos in the haunting refrain from the musical, *Fiddler on the Roof:* "Sunrise, sunset, swiftly fly the years/One season following another/Laden with happiness and tears." Indeed, for each of us the years fly swiftly by, and with Job we have to acknowledge, "Man is of few days."

Those few days, said Job, are "full of trouble." Once again this book confronts us with the fundamental fact that life will have its testings, troubles, and trials. As the Negro spiritual also reminds us, "All God's children got trouble."

But trouble can be wings to the soul, enabling us to reach higher heights and attainments. Many who have served the world best have suffered most. The greatest saints have often been the greatest sufferers. To live a holy life, to be filled with the Spirit, does not admit us into a charmed life that is trouble free. William Booth, founder of the Salvation Army, said in those days when his followers were suffering persecution, "It's our troubles that give us our anecdotes."

God does not promise us immunity from life's woes. But, as Annie Johnson Flint reminds us, He promises something better:

> God hath not promised skies always blue,
>   Flower-strewn pathways all our lives through:
> God hath not promised sun without rain,
>   Joy without sorrow, peace without pain.
> God hath not promised we shall not know
>   Toil and temptation, trouble and woe;
> He hath not told us we shall not bear,
>   Many a burden, many a care.
> But God hath promised strength for the day,
>   Rest for the labor, light for the way,
> Grace for the trials, help from above,
>   Unfailing sympathy, undying love.

Thank You, Lord, for the promise of Your presence, peace, and power in time of need.

Portrait Thirty-seven
LIFE AFTER DEATH? -1-

If a man dies, will he live again? (Job 14:14)

Job posed the universal question. The Hebrew conception of death was the cessation of being. There was no doctrine of immortality in Old Testament times. But Job dared to go beyond the strict limits of the traditional theology of his accusers and boldly asked: "If a man dies, will he live again?"

It is an ancient question, echoing across the centuries. It is a central question of history and life. Among the vast treasures of history, inscriptions on tombs of tribes extinct for centuries and remarkably preserved mummies offer mute testimony to man's ancient quest for immortality.

It is an anxious question. Job himself referred to death as "the king of terrors" (18:14) and a "journey of no return" (16:22). Shakespeare's Hamlet in his soliloquy echoed Job's sentiment in describing death as "the undiscover'd country from whose bourn no traveller returns." Death imposes for many a certain fear and anxiety. "Never send to know for whom the bell tolls," warned John Donne, preaching in St. Paul's nearly four centuries ago; "It tolls for thee!"

It is an argued question. Mind you, men do not argue with death, but about death. There have been endless speculations on its meaning and mystery. The atheist Feuerbach termed life after death "a wishful projection"; Marx called it a consolation for the oppressed; and Freud viewed it as an unrealistic regression of the psychologically immature.

For Job, to ask this very question was a leap of faith. The question of Job exposes his innate hope and quest for immortality. God has placed intimations of immortality all about us. William Jennings Bryan, in a sense, has given us an eloquent paraphrase of Job's question:

If the Father deigns to touch with divine power, the cold and pulseless heart of the buried acorn and make it burst forth from its prison walls, will He leave neglected in the earth the soul of a man made in the image of his Creator?

If He stoops to give to the rose bush whose withered blossoms float upon the autumn breeze the sweet assurance of another spring, will He refuse the words of hope to the sons of men when the frost of winter comes?

If matter, mute and inanimate, though changed by the forces of nature into a multitude of forms can never die, will the imperial spirit of man suffer annihilation when it has paid a brief visit like a royal guest to this tenement of clay?

Author and Sustainer of life, I thank You that You have not left this central question unanswered. Confirm in my heart the hope that I have in life after death through Jesus Christ our Lord.

Portrait Thirty-eight
LIFE AFTER DEATH? -2-

If a man dies, will he live again? (Job 14:14)

Job's question has been the riddle of the universe throughout the ages. He put into words the yearning sigh of all humanity. It is a question that the schools of philosophy cannot answer. It is beyond the realm of science and technology to answer it. With Mary of old, confronted with the stark fact of death, the mournful inquiry of humankind has been, "Who shall roll away the stone from the sepulcher?"

This ancient, anxious, and argued question finds its answer only in Christ. We must put this question alongside the words of our risen Lord who alone could declare with ultimate authority: "He who believes in Me will live, even though he dies" (John 11:25).

The resurrection of Christ once and for all indisputably answered the age-old question: "If a man dies, will he live again?" Men had been puzzled and perplexed by death. But Christ the Mighty Conqueror came and cut the Gordian knot of death by the all-powerful sword of His resurrection.

Because of His triumph over death, the grave has become the passage to immortality. It is but the robing room where we put aside the travel-worn attire of our earthly pilgrimage to become clothed in the garments of immortality. The name of Jesus will be our password at the gates of death to usher us into life eternal and the joys of heaven.

A retired army officer returned from India to spend his last days in England. One day his friends persuaded him to give an account of his life and services in India. They listened with breathless interest to the account of his illustrious military career. At the conclusion he said, "I expect to see something more thrilling than anything I have yet seen." His hearers were surprised since they knew he was well past seventy and retired from active service. After a pause he added in a reverent tone, "I refer to the first five minutes after death!"

Eternal Father, thank You that the end of time is eternity and that my last step leads into Your presence and the unspeakable joys You have prepared for me.

LONG-WINDED SPEECHES

Will your long-winded speeches never end? (Job 16:3)

Job was certainly not the first, and we can all attest that he was not the last, to be the victim of long-winded speeches. We have all suffered speakers who could not have said less unless they said more and who seemed, like Tennyson's brook, to go on forever! In his frustration with his friends' long, offensive orations, Job cried out, "Will your long-winded speeches never end?" This is another instance of the humor to be found in the Book of Job.

The speeches of Job's "comforters" would not be judged long by modern standards. But it was more the content than the length that made them seem so interminable to Job. Their speeches were insensitive, offensive, presumptuous, dogmatic—traits that would make any speech too long. Better a few words that help and heal than many that hinder and hurt.

Not merely speeches but conversation can be monopolized, one-sided, insensitive, egocentric, without the courtesy of good listening and sharing. We all need to pray the preacher's prayer, "Lord, fill my mouth with worthwhile stuff and stop me when I've said enough."

Job said, "If you were in my place . . . my mouth would encourage you; comfort from my lips would bring you relief" (16:4-5). Many people we meet every day are carrying heavy burdens, struggling with a heartache. They need our words of comfort, of encouragement, of affirmation.

There are said to be three narrow gates through which our words must pass. First, "Is it true?" Then, "Is it needful?" And the last and narrowest, "Is it kind?" If our words pass through these three gateways, we need not fear the results of our speech.

We are reminded in the Book of James that both good and bad words can come out of the same mouth (James 3:10). An anonymous poet has expressed it this way:

> A careless word may kindle strife;
> A cruel word may wreck a life;
> A bitter word may hate instill;
> A brutal word may smite and kill.
> A gracious word may smooth the way;
> A joyous word may light the day;
> A timely word may lessen stress
> A loving word may heal and bless.

Gracious Heavenly Father, with the psalmist I pray, "May the words of my mouth and the meditation of my heart be pleasing in Your sight" (Ps. 19:4).

THE JOURNEY OF NO RETURN

Only a few years will pass before I go on the journey of no return (Job 16:22).

Death and the brevity of life recurringly occupied Job's thinking and speaking. At that moment, it seemed that all that had been worthwhile in life was now behind him, and we hear his plaintive words, "Only a few years will pass before I go on the journey of no return."

For each of us, death will be a journey of no return. True, the believer will have an afterlife, but he can never again live the life given here on earth. We pass through this world but once. Someone has said that life is like a parachute jump—you have to get it right the first time.

In the flyleaf of my mother-in-law's Bible was written an epitaph that matched her saintly life: "What I spent, I had; what I gave, I have; what I kept, I lost." As we go through life on our one-time journey, it is only what we give that we will have for eternity.

That famous poet, "Anon," preaches to us of this truth:

The bread that bringeth strength I want to give,
The water pure that bids the thirsty live:
I want to help the fainting day by day;
I'm sure I shall not pass again this way.

I want to give to others hope and faith,
I want to do all that the Master saith;

I want to live aright from day to day,
I'm sure I shall not pass again this way.

Heavenly Father, help me to learn from the fable of the tortoise and the hare that the race is not always to the swift, so that I will slow down from life's fevered pace and take time for the priorities.

WHERE IS MY HOPE?

Where then is my hope? (Job 17:15)

If anyone's case seemed hopeless, it was Job's. Having lost everything he owned, his body tortured with pain and disfigurement, and now suffering the scorn of his peers, he cried out, "Where then is my hope? Who can see any hope for me?"

Job's cry echoes the need for all mankind. We need hope for our day-to-day living so that we will not succumb to despair or defeat. We need hope for eternity so that the grave is not the end of it all.

We of the New Testament era can look beyond the pages of Job to the One of whose coming Phillips Brooks penned: "The hopes and fears of all the years/Are met in Thee tonight." Christ came to be the Hope of the world. The Apostle Paul writes of "Christ in you, the hope of glory" (Col. 1:27). Life with Christ is an endless hope; without Him, a hopeless end.

Archimedes asked only for one fixed and immovable point which he said if he found, he could move the earth. So in life, each of us needs one point that is unshakably certain. Christ is that Archimedean point which can sustain the whole structure of life. He is the basis of all certainty. The words of Edward Mote's great hymn provide the anthem of hope for the Christian:

> My hope is built on nothing less
> Than Jesus' blood and righteousness,

I dare not trust the sweetest frame,
But wholly lean on Jesus' name.

When darkness seems to veil His face,
I rest on His unchanging grace;
In every high and stormy gale,
My anchor holds within the veil.

His oath, His covenant and blood,
Support me in the 'whelming flood;
When all around my soul gives way,
He then is all my hope and stay.

*God of hope, strengthen and confirm my hope in Christ so I
shall endure the hardships and finish in the great race of life.*

Portrait Forty-two

THE MEMORY WE LEAVE BEHIND

The memory of him perishes from the earth (Job 18:17).

Memory! What a world in a word! According to the poets, memory is given so we might have summer roses right through winter. Aristotle aptly described memory as the "scribe of the soul." Memory is one of God's great gifts to humankind.

Bildad, in one of the most eloquent passages in the Book of Job, described the wicked in the most graphic terms. He said of them:

> The lamp of the wicked is snuffed out;
> the flame of his fire stops burning.
> The light in his tent becomes dark;
> the lamp beside him goes out.
> The vigor of his step is weakened. . . .
> Calamity is hungry for him (18:5-12).

And then, almost as a climax, he stated, "The memory of him perishes from the earth; he has no name in the land" (18:17). Not to be remembered seemed to Bildad to be the nadir of calamities. For, after all, do we not all want to be remembered for good, to leave a legacy of a life that will bring blessings after we are gone?

This text of Job leads us to ask, "For what will I be remembered? Will it be for love, for integrity, for encouragement, for godliness, for faithfulness?" There is always the danger that a person can be remembered for selfishness, for unfaithfulness, for negative qualities.

Job is remembered for his steadfast faith that survived the worst that life could throw at him. May we live so close to God and maintain so strong a faith that the proverb in God's Word will be as our epitaph: "The memory of the righteous will be a blessing" (Prov. 10:7).

Father in heaven, help me not to disappoint those who look up to me but to so live today and tomorrow that the memory of my life will be a benediction to those I have loved and known.

Portrait Forty-three
THE WEALTH OF HEALTH

I am nothing but skin and bones (Job 19:20).

A number of our common expressions have come to us from the Book of Job. We already mentioned the humorous "long-winded speeches" (16:3). As Job pondered his emaciated body, he lamented, "I am nothing but skin and bones." Reduced to "skin and bones" has become synonymous with the loss of health. He then added the proverbial saying which many have used in a close brush with calamity: "I have escaped with only the skin of my teeth" (19:20).

The human body is one of the most remarkable creations of God. With the psalmist we acknowledge, "I am . . . wonderfully made" (Ps. 139:14). Centuries ago, Sophocles wrote: "Numberless are the world's wonders, but none—none more wondrous than the body of man." Augustine echoed the same theme:

Men go abroad to wonder at the height of mountains,
at the huge waves of the sea,
at the long courses of the rivers,
at the vast compass of the ocean,
at the circular motion of the stars;
and they pass by themselves without wondering.

Emerson said, "The greatest wealth is health." Next to having a good conscience, health is the most valued gift. We tend to be notoriously negligent in care of the treasure of the bodies God gives to us. We fail to give them due exercise, nutrition, and rest. In a sense, our bodies are our autobiographies. They tell on us whether we are indulgent or disciplined; whether we are living for pleasures of the flesh or for the glory of God.

The Apostle Paul, writing to the early church at Rome, but also to Christians of all ages, enjoined: "I urge you . . . to offer your bodies as living sacrifices, holy and pleasing to God—which is your spiritual worship" (Rom. 12:1). The dedication of our bodies to God is not something extraneous to our spiritual lives, but Paul declares it is part of our worship. In another letter, he states that he disciplines his body "so that after I have preached to others, I myself will not be disqualified for the prize" (1 Cor. 9:27).

As with Job, there are some physical infirmities beyond human control. But let us maximize our bodies' defenses and condition to be fit instruments for His service. Christ calls us to the pursuit of excellence, to be the best that we can be. Self-denial and the Cross are still inextricably interwoven with discipleship. Christ calls us from feasting to fasting, from the supper room to the Upper Room, from selfishness to sanctification. Let us rise up to the challenge of fully dedicated and disciplined lives.

Triune God, I yield to You the trinity of myself—my spirit, my mind, my body, for Your service and glory.

Portrait Forty-four
THE BLESSING OF BOOKS

Oh, that my words were recorded (Job 19:23).

Job's words could well be the text for aspiring authors when he sighed:

> Oh, that my words were recorded,
> that they were written on a scroll,
> that they were inscribed with an iron tool on lead,
> or engraved in rock forever (19:23-24).

Being involved in the publishing as well as the writing business, my staff reviews over 1,000 manuscripts a year. We are sensitive and empathetic to the deep yearning on the part of many to have their words recorded, to be published. As fellow philologers, lovers of words, we appreciate the value of the printed word.

For those of us who have fallen captive to the charm and magic of words, the Bible gives a proverb as a golden rule to strive for in one's speech and writing: "A word aptly spoken is like apples of gold in settings of silver" (Prov. 25:11). That striking simile pays a high compliment to the delights found on the picturesque paths of well-chosen words. A cat with a ball of yarn is a graceless thing compared to a craftsman with a fistful of words!

We are all incalculable debtors to the world of books. A good book is the best of friends. Francis Bacon reminds us that "reading maketh a full man." Abraham Cowley in the seventeenth century wrote:

> Ah, yet, ere I descend to the grave
> May I a small house and a large garden have,
> A few friends, and many books, both true,
> Both wise, and both delightful too!

Job's expressed longing for his words to be recorded, to be indelibly inscribed, has taken place beyond his wildest dreams. As has already been noted, the Book of Job is a masterpiece of literature. How like God that from the saddest story of the Bible, He brings the greatest humor, some of the most radiant texts, and the loftiest literature.

Books of blessing have often come from the crucible of suffering. Moses wrote the Pentateuch in the wilderness. David penned many of the psalms while being pursued by Saul. Isaiah lived in difficult days and died a martyr's death. Ezekiel wrote in exile. Jeremiah's life was one of trial and persecution. Peter wrote his two letters shortly before martyrdom. Paul dictated some of his epistles in prison. John gave us the magnificent Apocalypse while in the bleak circumstances of exile on the Isle of Patmos.

And what of God's modern penmen? John Bunyan wrote the greatest Christian classic from a prison cell. Dietrich Bonhoeffer's devotional classics and Corrie ten Boom's story came out of Hitler's death camps. Aleksandr Solzhenitsyn writing surreptitiously in his Russian prison camp and Joni Eareckson Tada as a quadriplegic from her wheelchair illustrate the inextinguishable spark for writing God's message under the most adverse circumstances. The Book of Job takes its place with the great Christian literature that has brought blessing out of barrenness, comfort out of chaos, thoroughfares out of life's troubles. How great is our God!

Living Word, thank You for the rich blessing and bounty of books, for the authors who have been to me Your instruments of insight and inspiration.

Portrait Forty-five
FROM PIT TO PINNACLE

I know that my Redeemer lives (Job 19:25).

Job rose from his pit of despair to his pinnacle of faith in the best-known and most-loved passage of this book. A shaft of brilliant sunlight broke through a rift in the clouds and he exclaimed:

> I know that my Redeemer lives,
> and that in the end He will stand upon the earth,
> and after my skin has been destroyed,
> yet in my flesh I will see God (19:25-26).

Job's testimony is one of the rare texts on immortality in the Old Testament and the most radiant. This textual jewel shines all the brighter because of its night-enshrouded setting. His staunch affirmation has been appropriated by Christians as we listen to the stirring soprano strains of Handel's *Messiah:* "I know that my Redeemer liveth."

W. Philip Keller, astute observer of nature, brings out a beautiful truth with an analogy. He points out that the trees growing above the timberline produce the most exquisite grain and resonant wood. These are the trees that endure the stresses and strains of being tossed and twisted by the wind and the wrenching fury of the storms. An extra flow of resin is produced in the trees which gives them the elegant grain and rare timbre and resonance not found in ordinary lumber cut at lower elevations. The strain of survival in an austere setting produces fibers for the finest musical instruments from which will come the melodies that will enrich a thousand listeners in Lincoln Center and encircle the globe to inspire a million more. Keller states the same principle is true for us as God's people (*Sky Edge*, Word, 1987, pp. 85-86). The choicest saints, whose lives have the most beautiful texture and who give the world its most inspiring songs, are those produced under the strains of adversity. Job, of course, is the classic example.

Suffering never leaves us where it finds us. Robert Schuller has said, "Life's suffering is a passage, not a cul-de-sac." Job's suffering led him to one of the most lofty affirmations found in the Bible. For each of us, our trials and sorrows can become a passage to a deeper trust, a more steadfast faith, and a closer relationship with God. God can lift us from pit to pinnacle, from depths to height, from being a victim to a victor amidst life's struggles and sorrows.

Gracious God, thank You that our extremity becomes Your opportunity to lift us, to enable us to find a song in our suffering and a triumph in our trial.

Portrait Forty-six
MY REDEEMER

I know that my Redeemer lives (Job 19:25).

There are some 100 radiant names and titles of our Lord in Scripture. Job, in his lofty affirmation of faith, introduced us to one of the most beautiful and meaningful of those titles ascribed to Christ as he testified, "I know that my Redeemer lives."

Quoting from my book, *100 Portraits of Christ*, that includes a chapter on this title of Christ:

> The Hebrew word *goel* [for Redeemer] represented the kinsman whose duty it was to recover a captured or enslaved relative. . . . This word in its original meaning also meant that the kinsman would recover sold or forfeited inheritance. He was the chief defender not only of the person but also of the possessions of the one over whom he was a protector. This was a part of the Mosaic Code.
>
> The loss of paradise was for man a tragedy. Sin made him forfeit his spiritual inheritance; it disenfranchised him of his heavenly citizenship; it robbed him of his nobility; it left him a miserable pauper. But Christ as our Redeemer has recovered our lost estate for us if we will accept His act of redemption. He is the Elder Brother, our great Kinsman, who undertook to win back for us that which we had lost (Henry Gariepy, *100 Portraits of Christ*, Victor Books, 1987, pp. 113-114).

Job's utterance was prophetic of the work of redemption for each of us. We of the Christian era, who are children of the Resurrection, can with much greater meaning testify, "I know that my Redeemer lives." As Elton Trueblood has aptly expressed it: "Faith is not a blind leap into nothing, but a thoughtful walk in the light we have." Job walked in the light that he had and was given a spiritual perception that anticipated the Redeemer of centuries to come.

The word *Redeemer* is not found in the New Testament. But the work done by the Redeemer is prominently proclaimed throughout its pages. Speaking of His coming again, Christ said, "When these things begin to take place, stand up and lift up your heads, because your redemption is drawing near" (Luke 21:28). The Apostle Paul wrote of the redemptive work of Christ in glowing terms: "For He has rescued us from the dominion of darkness and brought us into the kingdom of the Son He loves, in whom we have redemption, the forgiveness of sins" (Col. 1:13-14).

What a rich and radiant title Job gave to us of our Lord, its meaning infinitely amplified by His supreme sacrifice on Calvary. With brothers and sisters of the faith, we join in the jubilant song of Philip Bliss:

I will sing of my Redeemer,
And His wondrous love to me;
On the cruel cross He suffered
From the curse to set me free.

Sing, O sing of my Redeemer,
With His blood He purchased me,
On the cross He sealed my pardon,
Paid the debt and made me free.

I will tell the wondrous story,
How my lost estate to save,
In His boundless love and mercy,
He the ransom freely gave.

Christ, my Redeemer, thank You for rescuing me from sin and recovering my lost heritage from God.

Portrait Forty-seven

THE GREATEST EVENT

He will stand upon the earth (Job 19:25).

"While I was walking on the moon" are the words with which astronaut James Irwin sometimes begins his talk. What could be a more arresting opening? You just have to hear what comes next!

Many have heard Colonel Irwin relate how he stood on the moon and saw Planet Earth suspended in space as an iridescent jewel. As a guest speaker at one of our programs, he shared that as he walked the thought came to him—"Man walking on the moon—this is the greatest event of human history!" And then it was he heard an inner voice speak to his heart, "I did something greater than that—I walked on the earth!"

Colonel Irwin testifies that he returned from the moon not to be a celebrity but a servant of the Lord of the universe who came and walked on the earth in the person of Jesus Christ.

Each Christmas we celebrate the greatest event of human history—the Incarnation—God taking on Himself the form of human flesh. Deity clothed in the garb of humanity. The Infinite becoming the Intimate. The Sovereign becoming the Saviour. That is why all the world has such a grand celebration. As Malcolm Muggeridge has expressed it: "The coming of Jesus into the world is the most stupendous event of human history."

"He will stand upon the earth"—this remarkable declaration of Job anticipated centuries in advance our Lord's coming to earth, the supreme event of history. For Job, it was his great hope. It enabled him to endure and maintain his faith amidst the fiercest assaults on him.

We live not with a great anticipation but with a grand realization. Our Redeemer has come to earth, and our lives can never again be the same. Because Christ came and He lives and reigns, we can face tomorrow. Because He came and through the power of His resurrection, we can say with even greater confidence than did Job, "And after my skin has been destroyed, yet in my flesh I will see God" (19:26).

God Incarnate, thank You for making the long journey from creation to our planet, for loving me, and Your amazing sacrifice of dying for me.

Portrait Forty-eight
OUR LORD'S RETURN -1-

In the end He will stand upon the earth (Job 19:25).

With remarkable spiritual insight and inspired foresight, Job spoke prophetically of the end times, stating, "I know that my Redeemer lives, and that in the end He will stand upon the earth."

Our Lord's return is one of the cardinal teachings of the Bible. Of the 260 chapters of the New Testament, 216 of them make reference to His coming again. No less than one of every thirty verses, twenty-three of the twenty-seven New Testament books, and all nine authors herald the thrilling and tumultuous truth of His return. Fifty times in his thirteen epistles, Paul spoke of this grand climax to all of history. Its sheer frequency in the New Testament underscores it as a paramount proclamation.

The great creeds of the church incorporate the tenet of His return. Our hymns exult in its anticipation with 5,000 of Charles Wesley's 7,000 hymns referring to it. In our day, the Gaithers have lyricized for the world to sing, "The King is coming!" All prophecies point toward this one grand event, the culmination of all evangelism and history.

Thus, Job became the Neil Armstrong of faith exploration, taking a giant step. He went on to say:

> Yet in my flesh I will see God;
> I myself will see Him with my own eyes—

I, and not another.
How my heart yearns within me! (19:26-27)

If Job, with his limited knowledge of our Lord's return, could express this yearning, how much more for us who have known His mighty life, His infinite sacrifice, His unfailing love and grace. May we have a deep yearning for that day when we shall look into His face and see our Saviour and the Lord of glory. It will be the greatest moment of our lives!

Dear Lord, thank You for Your gracious and glorious promise that You will come again, and when You do, You will receive me unto Yourself so that where You are there I may be also.

Portrait Forty-nine

OUR LORD'S RETURN -2-

In the end He will stand upon the earth (Job 19:25).

We continue with this extraordinary text on eschatology from the Book of Job. Refuting the belief of his time that there was no life after death, he unequivocally affirmed that he would see God after death. As a non-Israelite, and without the promises of God, he yet proclaimed the coming of the Redeemer to earth in the end time.

His prophetical words of our Lord's coming to earth can refer to either His incarnation or His second coming. Both, from Job's standpoint, represent the Redeemer on the earth, either the time of Christ's first coming or His return in mighty triumph.

During the first World War, a soldier in the trenches saw his friend wounded out in no-man's-land, that ground between his trench and that of the enemy. The man asked his officer, "May I go and bring him back?" The officer refused. "If you go, I would lose you as well. I have to say no." But, disobeying the officer, he went out to save his friend. He managed to bring his friend back, only to fall mortally wounded as he staggered to his trench. The officer was angry. "I told you not to go. Now I have lost two good men. It was not worth it." With his dying breath the man said, "But it *was* worth it, Sir, because when I got to him, he said, 'Jim, I knew you'd come.' "

It was unspeakable love that brought Christ from heaven to

earth on that first Advent and then led Him to go forth to the "no-man's-land" of Calvary, there to be wounded to the death that He might bring us back from death to life, from defeat to victory, from sin to salvation. The grand and glorious message of the Gospel is that in the midst of the world's greatest battle, Jesus will come!

Jesus is coming again! He comes to bring us safely to Himself. May we be able to look up into His face and, knowing Him as Saviour and Friend, say, "Lord Jesus, I knew You'd come!"

Christ, whose promises are sure, help me to be found ready at Your coming, to welcome You as One long known and loved, to hear Your, "Well done, good and faithful servant."

Portrait Fifty

I WILL SEE GOD

In my flesh I will see God (Job 19:26).

Job once again took a quantum leap of faith as he exclaimed, "In my flesh I will see God; I myself will see Him with my own eyes—I, and not another." This text is the greatest testimony on immortality in the Old Testament.

In the United States, the highest and lowest elevations are in remarkably close proximity—Death Valley (282' below sea level) and Mount McKinley (20,320' above sea level). The same God who created the lowest and highest points on this hemisphere almost next to each other also gave us man's lowest and highest points in the Bible right next to each other here in the Book of Job. Man's loftiest testimony on life after death comes right after his lowest depths of despair. How like God to plumb man's most radiant testimony from the depths of his sorrow and tragedy.

It boggles the mind to contemplate what it will be like to see God. The majesty, magnificence, and awesomeness of that experience defies any possible description. It will be the quintessence of all human experience, an event nonpareil in the range of human experience.

Our hymnals anticipate this experience. One favorite that captures the wonder of this anticipation is Grant Tullar's:

> Face to face with Christ, my Saviour,
> Face to face, what will it be?

When with rapture I behold Him,
Jesus Christ who died for me.

Face to face I shall behold Him,
Far beyond the starry sky;
Face to face in all His glory,
I shall see Him by and by!

In that magnificent Book of Revelation, John described the eternal joys of heaven. He told of the resurrection and reign of saints, the rule of the Saviour, the New Jerusalem, the New Heaven and the New Earth, and the Ten "No Mores" of eternity. But John had learned from his Master—He kept the best wine till last. The culmination of all the glories of heaven, its *ne plus ultra*, heaven's crowning joy will be—"They will see His face" (Rev. 22:4).

John elsewhere wrote to the churches, "When He appears . . . we shall see Him as He is" (1 John 3:2). The seer has written of the eternal destiny of the believer: "Now the dwelling of God is with men, and He will live with them. They will be His people, and God Himself will be with them and be their God" (Rev. 21:3). There is nothing in all Scripture that parallels this glorious blessing to be bestowed by God on men.

Poet laureate Lord Tennyson has expressed it in immortal words that he requested appear at the end of any of his published poems:

For tho' from out our bourne of Time and Place
   the flood may bear me far,
I hope to see my Pilot face to face
   when I have crossed the bar.

Heavenly Father, my highest and holiest aspiration is to someday behold Your glory and live with You forever.

Portrait Fifty-one

WHY DO THE WICKED PROSPER?

Why do the wicked live on, growing old and increasing in power? (Job 21:7)

We often hear the question "Why do bad things happen to good people?" The other side of that coin is, "Why do good things happen to bad people?"

Zophar eloquently presented his case (Job 20) that the wicked suffer misfortune. He said to Job, "Surely you know how it has been from of old, ever since man was placed on the earth, that the mirth of the wicked is brief, the joy of the godless lasts but a moment" (20:4-5). In graphic language, Zophar declared that the pride and prosperity of the wicked quickly vanish and come to naught—"His prosperity will not endure. . . . Distress will overtake him. . . . Such is the fate God allots the wicked," concludes Zophar (20:21-29).

However, Job bought none of it. In the next chapter (21), he derided Zophar's argument. He asked, "Have you never questioned those who travel? . . . That the evil man is spared from the day of calamity?" (21:29-30) Job made his case by pointing out that the wicked are not always overtaken with distress: "Their homes are safe and free from fear. . . . Their bulls never fail to breed; their cows calve and do not miscarry. . . . Their children . . . sing to the music of tambourine and harp. . . . They spend their years in prosperity and go down to the grave in peace" (21:9-13). Job chidingly concluded, "So how can you console me with your nonsense? Nothing is left of your answers but falsehood!" (21:34)

The answer to this question as revealed in the Book of Job is that we are living on a depraved planet, a part of the universe occupied by the rebel. Temporarily, wrong may prosper and good may suffer, but God ultimately will balance the ledgers. This is warmly illustrated in the following story.

Theodore Roosevelt was coming home from Africa where he had been hunting big game. When he boarded the ship at the African port, they rolled out the red carpet for him. Crowds gathered on the dock and cheered him. On board, he was given the finest suite, and during the voyage he was the center of interest.

Another man boarded the ship at the same time. He was an old missionary who had given his life for Christ in Africa. Now his wife was dead, his children gone. Aged and worn out, he was returning to America. But no one noticed him; no one showed interest in him.

When the ship docked at San Francisco, a great crowd greeted Mr. Roosevelt. The bells rang, the whistles blew, and again they rolled out the red carpet. He landed amid pomp and glory. But no one was there to meet the missionary. No one noticed him. He went to a small hotel to spend the night.

That evening he knelt by the side of the bed and prayed, "Lord, I am not complaining, but I just don't understand. I gave my life for You in Africa, but it seems that no one cares. Lord, I just don't understand." And, in that moment, it seemed that the Lord reached down from heaven and laid His hand on the old man's shoulder and said, "Missionary, you're not home yet."

Righteous Father, who sends Your rain on the just and on the unjust, confirm my faith that You will bring in the day when righteousness shall reign and sin and evil shall be no more.

AT PEACE WITH GOD

Submit to God and be at peace with Him (Job 22:21).

Job's three would-be comforters continued to discourse on their one theme. Tradition must be defended, even at the expense of truth. They continued to dogmatize on their major premise that virtue brings fortune; sin brings misfortune.

However, as we continue to discover on our safari through Job, their eloquent orations contain some sparkling gems of truth. As Eliphaz started the third and final round of the debate, believing that Job's suffering was the result of sin, he urged, "Submit to God and be at peace with him." We have no problem with his theology on that statement. Peace with God comes when we surrender to His will for us.

Peace is the great pursuit of humankind today. Our world, torn and tortured by conflict and wars, longs and prays for peace. The human race today sits under a nuclear sword of Damocles. All it will take is for some moral infant to push a button, and we will perish in instant apocalypse.

In his bestseller, *Peace of Mind*, Joshua Liebman tells of his experience as a young man. He listed the supreme goods in his life and took them to a wise mentor. When he showed him the list, he expected to be praised for his precocity. His list included such values as love, health, riches, talent, beauty, friends. The wise old mentor pondered the list, and then with a twinkle in his eye, reached for a pencil. He drew a line through each item on the list and then said, "Young man, you may have all of these, but they will turn out to be your enemies instead of friends unless you have the one and most important thing you missed." Then he wrote on the paper: "The gift of an untroubled mind."

Thoreau's words are more true of our generation than of his, when over a century ago he wrote, "The mass of men lead lives of quiet desperation." The gift of an untroubled mind comes from God. The Prophet Isaiah gives us the precious promise: "You will keep him in perfect peace, whose mind is stayed on You, because he trusts in You" (Isa. 26:3, NKJV).

There is a sense in which the world can give peace to a man. It is when there is an absence of danger, no financial worries, and a sense of physical well-being and mental contentment. But such peace is dependent on exterior circumstances. It is fragile and can easily be lost with the approach of difficulty and danger.

But there is a peace that the world cannot know and cannot give. It is the deep abiding peace within the heart, irrespective of external circumstances. When Jesus promised, "My peace I give to you" (John 14:27), it was in a setting of trouble and turmoil. The air of the city outside that Upper Room where He spoke those words was electric with the storm that was about to burst on Him in all its fury. Outside those doors awaited the shadows and agony of Gethsemane, treason from the ranks of His trusted friends, the mockery of the trials, and the ignominy of Calvary. Yet we hear His calm words and legacy to His followers of all ages: "My peace I give you. I do not give to you as the world gives. Do not let your hearts be troubled and do not be afraid" (John 14:27).

In His will is our peace. Paul described it as "the peace . . . that transcends all understanding" (Phil. 4:7).

> *God of peace, free me from all worry and anxiety that would*
> *be a badge of my unbelief, and let Your peace rule in my heart.*

THE RICHEST MAN

The Almighty will be your gold (Job 22:25).

Once again Eliphaz came up with a statement of truth that has application to our day. He was addressing the one who had been the wealthiest man in the East. Many of us in our own society are so glutted with luxuries that we have forgotten how to enjoy our necessities. The words spoken by Eliphaz would make a good watchword for today: "The Almighty will be your gold, the choicest silver for you."

We need to differentiate between true wealth and what most people consider as wealth. True wealth is not money, possessions, luxuries, security. Those things that glitter will someday turn to dust and ashes in our hands. True wealth consists in such spiritual treasures as love, peace, faith, friends, service, wisdom. As stated in our text, God is our true wealth.

A rich man named Carl loved to ride his horse through his vast estate to congratulate himself on his wealth. One day on such a ride, he came on Hans, an old tenant farmer who had sat down to eat his lunch in the shade of a great oak tree.

Hans' head was bowed in prayer. When he looked up, he said, "Oh, excuse me, Sir. I didn't see you. I was giving thanks for my food."

"Hmph!" snorted Carl, noticing the coarse dark bread and cheese constituting the old man's lunch. "If that were all I had to eat, I don't think I would feel like giving thanks."

"Oh," replied Hans, "it is quite sufficient. But it is remarkable that you should come by today, Sir. I . . . I feel I should tell you, I had a strange dream just before awakening this morning."

"And what did you dream?" Carl asked with an amused smile.

"It seemed there was beauty and peace all around, and yet I could hear a voice saying, 'The richest man in the valley will die tonight.'"

"Dreams!" cried the landowner. "Nonsense!" And he turned and galloped away.

"Lord, have mercy on his soul if he really is to die so soon," Hans prayed as he watched horse and rider disappear.

Die tonight, mused Carl. It was ridiculous, of course! No use his going into a panic. The best thing to do about the old man's dream was to forget it.

But he couldn't forget it. He had felt fine, at least until Hans described his stupid dream. Now he didn't feel too well.

That evening he called his doctor, who was also a personal friend. "Could you come over?" he asked. "I need to talk to you."

When the doctor arrived, Carl told him the whole story. "Sounds like poppycock to me," the doctor said, "but for your peace of mind, let's examine you."

A little later, his examination complete, the doctor was full of assurances. "Carl, you're as strong and healthy as that horse of yours. There's no way you're going to die tonight." Carl thanked his friend and told him how foolish he felt for being upset by an old man's dream.

It was about 9 A.M. when a messenger arrived at Carl's door. "It's old Hans," the messenger said. "He died last night in his sleep."

The richest man in our Bible drama was not among those who trusted in earthly possessions. It was the one who, although bereft of all worldly goods, held on to his integrity and faith in God.

Heavenly Father, deliver me from life's phantom charms, and those things that would possess me, that I may ever seek first Your kingdom and righteousness, which alone will make life rich and great.

A PRAYER-ANSWERING GOD

You will pray to Him, and He will hear you (Job 22:27).

Before we let Eliphaz depart from the scene, let us ponder one more timeless truth he uttered in his final words to Job. He voiced a statement that is a foundation truth for the believer: "Pray to Him [God] and He will hear you."

Modern life, it seems, is consumed in a tornado of activity, a torrent of voices, a tumult of noise. We need to find each day a sanctuary of solitude where we may replenish our spent resources, a place of quiet where we can hear the accents of the Eternal. Wordsworth's words are still apt:

The world is too much with us; late and soon,
Getting and spending, we lay waste our powers.

Job needed the strengthening that comes through prayer. We need the power of prayer for our daily living, tasks, and struggles. As Paul Rees expresses it, "Nothing lies outside the reach of prayer except that which lies outside the will of God."

Prayer is pivotal for the believer. We will be better or worse as we pray more or less. In prayer, our weakness is linked to the Almighty, our ignorance to God's wisdom, and our finite self to the Infinite God. Prayer is the intimate companion of consecration.

"He who has learned to pray," declared William Law, "has

learned the greatest secret of a holy and happy life." True prayer is a secret, an art. Prayer may well be the most difficult discipline for the Christian. Oh, yes, there is a prayer that is easy—superficial prayer, the repetition of phrases, coming hurriedly to God with preoccupied minds, tired bodies, and restless spirits. Such activity is not true prayer.

Only as we near the end of the Book of Job, where there is a real communion with God, does Job emerge triumphant in his trial. When he stops talking and starts listening to God, a dramatic transformation takes place. It is ever so with the children of God.

Let us put into practice our belief that we have a prayer-hearing and prayer-answering God.

I have often had to conform my prayer to the words composed by John Greenleaf Whittier:

> Dear Lord and Father of mankind,
>   Forgive our foolish ways;
> Reclothe us in our rightful mind;
> In purer lives Thy service find,
>   In deeper reverence, praise.
>
> Drop Thy still dews of quietness
>   Till all our strivings cease;
> Take from our souls the strain and stress,
> And let our ordered lives confess
>   The beauty of Thy peace.

Portrait Fifty-five
FINDING GOD

If only I knew where to find Him (Job 23:3).

Through the ages, man has longed to know God. Augustine expressed the yearning of all humankind when he said, "O God, our hearts are restless until they find their rest in Thee." Job, out of the depths of his suffering and despair, cried, "If only I knew where to find Him." He went on to say that he knew God would deal justly with him, and he would be delivered from the false accusations against him.

How do we find God? Job acknowledged that no matter where we may look, we cannot find Him—"But if I go to the east, He is not there; if I go to the west, I do not find Him. When He is at work in the north, I do not see Him; when He turns to the south, I catch no glimpse of Him" (23:8-9). God leaves no footprints in the sand, no fingerprints on our doorknob, no traces of His coming and going. How can we find Him?

Job's longing had to wait until "the Word became flesh and lived for a while among us" (John 1:14). That same Word declared, "I am the way and the truth and the life. No one comes to the Father except through Me." Hearing this, the disciple Philip said, "Lord, show us the Father and that will be enough for us." Jesus answered, "Anyone who has seen Me has seen the Father" (John 14:6-9). Thus, the New Testament gives the glowing answer to Job's question. The way to find God is through Christ.

Through Christ we come to know the love of God, the salvation of God, the power of God, and His gift of life eternal.

But, in another sense, God was round about Job. He was aware of his suffering. He had sustained his faith and would vindicate his integrity. Before the book concludes, God Himself comes to Job and speaks to him as He did to no other person in the Bible. So when it seems God is distant, let us remember He is never far away, and that He is keeping watch above His own. The next verse we will consider reassures us of that comforting truth.

Christ the Way, lead me to the Father that finding Him I may know Him, knowing Him I may love Him, and loving Him I may do His holy will.

Portrait Fifty-six
HE KNOWS

But He knows the way that I take (Job 23:10).

Job now testified that though he could not by searching find God, God knew him and the way he was going. In one of the most affirming verses in this book, Job testified, "He knows the way that I take." What a blessed assurance this verse has for us today.

He knows. He knows the storms that buffet our lives. He knows the trials that we must endure. He knows the afflictions that come into our lives. He knows the cross we are called to carry. He knows the path we must travel. He knows, and he understands, and He will be by our side to help and sustain.

It is an incredible thought, that the Creator and Governor of the universe knows me and the way that I take. It is a comforting thought, that the One who holds the stars on their unerring courses holds my finite life in His mighty hands. Stanley E. Ditmer has expressed this comforting thought in his words that have sung their way around the world:

> I shall not fear though darkened clouds may
>   gather round me;
> The God I serve is one who cares and understands.
> Although the storms I face would threaten to
>   confound me,
> Of this I am assured: I'm in His hands.

I'm in His hands, I'm in His hands;
Whate'er the future holds
   I'm in His hands,
The days I cannot see
Have all been planned for me;
His way is best, you see;
   I'm in His hands.

What though I cannot know the way that
   lies before me?
I still can trust and freely follow His commands;
My faith is firm since it is He that watches
   o'er me;
Of this I'm confident: I'm in His hands.

*Eternal God, thank You for the assurance that You know the
way of my life and that I am in Your love and care.*

Portrait Fifty-seven

GOLD FEARS NO FIRE

When He has tested me, I will come forth as gold (Job 23:10).

In Job's declaration of innocence, he appealed to the supreme tribunal in one of the most beautiful verses of the book: "But He knows the way that I take; when He has tested me, I will come forth as gold." Faith is the golden shield of the Christian, and gold fears no fire!

"The caliber of a man," writes Thomas Kelly, "is found in his ability to meet disappointment successfully, enriched rather than narrowed by it." Job's faith was tested to its limits. But as gold tested by fire comes out pure and undiminished, so Job came through his furnace of affliction with a faith that was refined and purified.

As fire reveals the purity of gold, so affliction reveals the purity of a life. The fire does not change gold but exposes the substance already there. Trial and affliction similarly bring out the quality already present in a life. As pure gold shines all the brighter when put to the fire, so faith glows the more radiant when put to the fiery test. In the end, Job's faith and trust, which already had made him a model in God's sight, enabled him to "come forth as gold."

The Arabs have a proverb: "All sunshine makes a desert." (They ought to know.) When life is easy, it is possible to live on the surface of things. But when trial and sorrow come, then one is driven to the deeper things. Then one can enter into the secrets and beauties of God. It is in the storm that

God arches His rainbow over us, its multi-splendor revealing all the elements of color that make up the beauty of the world. Life's greatest revelations come in its storms.

"God never wastes suffering," writes Warren Wiersbe. He adds, "Trials work for us, not against us. . . . God permits trials that He might build character into our lives. He can grow a mushroom overnight, but it takes many years—and many storms—to build a mighty oak" (*A Time to Be Renewed*, Victor Books, 1986, p. 49).

> *Heavenly Father, give me a faith and trust that will be*
> *equal to the testings and trials of life, so that like Job, though I be*
> *tried as with fire, I will come forth as gold.*

Portrait Fifty-eight

THE GROANS OF THE DYING

The groans of the dying rise from the city (Job 24:12).

In Job 24, Job, in further rebuttal of his disputants' creed, complained of the unfairness of life and man's inhumanity to man. He vividly described ruthless cheating and theft: "Men move boundary stones; they pasture flocks they have stolen. They drive away the orphan's donkey and take the widow's ox in pledge" (24:2-3). He lamented the lot of the hungry and the homeless and spoke of baby snatching: "The fatherless child is snatched from the breast; the infant of the poor is seized for a debt" (24:9).

Adultery is committed under cover of darkness (24:15). Evil and violence are rampant, and Job's words are filled with pathos: "The groans of the dying rise from the city, and the souls of the wounded cry out for help" (24:12).

Have we not heard the groans of the dying and the cries of the wounded in our day? Have not the groans reached our ears of the millions starving in Ethiopia and destitute parts of our world? Do we not hear the cries of the 1½ million fetuses killed each year in the U.S. in the silent holocaust of abortion? And can we neglect the plight of the hungry and homeless all around us in affluent America?

And have not our consciences been seared by what is perhaps man's greatest inhumanity to man in all of history—the Holocaust? The question haunts us: "How could God allow 6 million of His 'chosen people' to be savaged?" Elie Wiesel, in his book *Night* (Bantam), painfully describes the Jews in his village being herded together, stripped of their possessions, and loaded into cattle cars. He saw his mother, young sister, and all his family disappear into an oven fueled with human flesh. He witnessed babies pitchforked, children hanged, and he himself narrowly escaped death. He writes of the first time he smelled the scent of burning humans: "Never shall I forget that night, seven times cursed and seven times sealed. Never shall I forget that smoke. Never shall I forget the little faces of the children, whose bodies I saw turned into wreaths of smoke beneath a silent blue sky. Never shall I forget those moments which murdered my God."

Today at the Protestant Chapel on the grounds of the Dachau death camp is another man who survived the Holocaust. This man, Christian Reger, spent four years as a prisoner in Dachau. His crime? He, along with Dietrich Bonhoeffer and others, resisted and spoke out against Hitler's heinous crimes. Today his mission is telling others that God's love is deeper than the pits of human depravity. He witnesses: "Here at Dachau, I learned something far greater than the 'why' of life. I learned to know the who of my life. He was enough to sustain me then, and is enough to sustain me still."

Christian Reger, and the Book of Job, teach us two lessons on this subject. Those who go through the deepest depths of suffering can know a divine presence who will stand with them and give an inner strength. And those of us who hear the groans of the dying and the cries of the wounded have a responsibility to apply the love and healing of Christ to our troubled and tortured world.

Where the world is at its worst, there the church of Jesus Christ should be at its best.

God, our Refuge and Strength, help me to serve my present age, to be a cup of strength to those who suffer, a light to those in darkness and despair.

Portrait Fifty-nine

WORM THEOLOGY

A son of man, who is only a worm! (Job 25:6)

This pessimistic and despondent assessment of man was spoken by Bildad. It is obviously an exaggeration to compare sinful man with a righteous and pure God (25:1-6). But regrettably, a "worm theology" has crept, or should we say "crawled," into the thinking of some. Jonathan Edwards, in his sermon on the damnation of sinners in 1734, described man as "a little, wretched, despicable creature; a worm, a mere nothing, and less than nothing; a vile insect that has risen up in contempt against the majesty of heaven and earth." And in our hymnals we find the words of Isaac Watts: "Did He devote that sacred head for such a worm as I?"

A difficult metaphor for an age caught up in self-esteem. Perhaps we have swung the pendulum too far in almost deifying humankind. True, a worm theology is a travesty on God's creation of man in His own image. But we live in an era that must beware of creating God in man's own image.

Our perspective has a tremendous advantage over Bildad. We are enlightened by the Incarnation. The fact that God sent His Son to live and die for us puts an infinite value on our souls. God honored the human race in the miracle of the manger. God Himself, in the person of Christ, as described by Milton, "Forsook the courts of everlasting day/And chose with us a darksome house of mortal clay." We are each somebody very special for God to do that for us.

It was the preacher of Ecclesiastes who proclaimed that life is "Meaningless! . . . Utterly meaningless" (Ecc. 1:2). But, his famous phrase, "under the sun," used some thirty times, is a clue to why he thought that way. He was dealing from an earthbound horizon. His observations were from ground level. We need the vertical perspective, the revelation of God to discern the true worth of man. Then we discover that we are children of God, heirs to an eternal destiny that surpasses our most daring imaginations.

Longfellow has expressed it for us in his celebrated lines:

> Tell me not, in mournful numbers,
> Life is but an empty dream!—
> For the soul is dead that slumbers,
> And things are not what they seem.
>
> Life is real! Life is earnest!
> And the grave is not its goal;
> Dust thou art, to dust returnest,
> Was not spoken of the soul.

Let us leave Bildad's outlook buried in the ground where it belongs, and let us rise to our God-appointed destiny!

Enable me, Lord, to see dawn beyond dusk, star above mist, and eternity beyond time.

Portrait Sixty
NAKED DEATH

Death is naked before God (Job 26:6).

Euripedes, the poet, called death "the debt we all must pay." The Arabs have a saying that "death is a black camel which kneels beside every man's gate." The invincible reaper knocks ultimately at every door. If he hasn't visited your family yet, watch the road.

Another Arab proverb says, "There are no pockets in a shroud." When we come to death, we leave everything behind. All we bring before our Maker is ourselves, our faith, and our character. Job announced this truth in our text: "Death is naked before God." He had earlier conceded: "Naked I came from my mother's womb, and naked will I depart'" (1:21). The same truth is preached in Ecclesiastes: "Naked a man comes from his mother's womb, and as he comes, so he departs" (5:15).

The bottom line of life and death is that it is not what we have but what we are that will count for eternity. When we appear before God, we will be stripped of all the things of earth. Left behind will be any plaques, possessions, portfolios, perquisites, prestige—all the bounty of a lifetime of collecting and gathering. Even persons nearest to us will not be there as we stand before God.

But there is one thing that we can take with us and that will make the difference. Death does not separate us from it. We can come before God in the grace of our Lord and Saviour

133

Jesus Christ. We will have no merit of our own, but in grace, the unmerited favor bestowed on us at Calvary, redeemed before His throne we shall stand. If we have known the grace of Christ and have faithfully served Him, then we shall hear His, "Well done."

The story is told of two strangers, a small boy and an older man, fishing on the banks of the Mississippi. As time passed, they discovered that, though the fishing was poor, conversation was good. By the time the sun began to sink in the west, they had talked of many things. At dusk, a large riverboat was seen moving slowly in the distance. When the boy saw the boat, he began to shout and wave his arms to attract the attention of those on board. The man watched and then said, "Son, that boat is not going to stop for you. It's on its way to some unknown place down the river and it surely won't stop for a small boy."

But suddenly the boat began to slow down, and it moved toward the riverbank. To the man's amazement, the boat came near enough to the shore that a gangplank could be lowered. The boy entered the boat and, turning to his new friend on shore, said, "Mister, I knew the boat would stop for me, for you see, my father is captain of this boat, and we're going to a new home down the river."

When the ship of death stops for the child of God, we can be confident that it is our Father who has called home one of His precious children. Death is not the end of life but the beginning of the larger, eternal life that awaits those who love and serve God.

And though we come before God shorn of all earth's trinkets, we can bring to death the treasure of our relationship as children of our Heavenly Father. God Himself promises: "To all who received Him, to those who believed in His name, He gave the right to become children of God" (John 1:12).

Heavenly Father, thank You that Your grace is the answer for the riddle of death and for Your assurance that this tenement of clay shall be transformed into a new and glorified body that shall abide with You forever.

THE SECRET OF SEEING

He suspends the earth over nothing (Job 26:7).

Job, in his reply to Bildad, rose to lofty eloquence on the subject of God's creation and exclaimed: "He spreads out the northern skies over empty space; He suspends the earth over nothing" (26:7).

Pulitzer Prize winner Annie Dillard has expressed this in modern lyrical lines: "After the one extravagant gesture of Creation in the first place, the universe has continued to deal exclusively in extravagance, flinging intricacies and colossi down aeons of emptiness." She further writes, "The secret of seeing is, then, the pearl of great price" (*Pilgrim at Tinker Creek*, Harper & Row, pp. 9, 33). Job had found the secret of seeing. He did not have a telescope, nor did he voyage into outer space. But, he had a spiritual discernment so that when he gazed at the star-strewn spaces of the heavens, he recognized the sublime signature of the Creator.

Poet E. Ruth Glover also discovered the "secret of seeing":

Across the blackness of the midnight sky
He lit a billion stars and hung them high;
And He who sets His candles in the night—
Will fill my dark and saddened heart with light.

And o'er the parching land His heaven pours
A trillion drops and countless more;

And He whose rivers reach toward the sea
Will put a fresh and flowing stream in me.

If Job were filled with awe and reverence at his observations
of the heavens, what would have been his exclamation if he
had been exposed to what we have seen and known? His
description of God who "suspends the earth over nothing"
was an imaginative expression far ahead of his time. Our
knowledge of this cosmic phenomenon has been incredibly
enhanced by modern astronomy. Our space technology has
captured in a stunningly beautiful photograph our Planet
Earth, as an iridescent jewel, suspended in the heavens. The
psalmist in his longing after God expressed an affinity with
Job's reverent contemplation: "My soul thirsts for God, for the
living God. Where can I go and meet with God? . . . Deep
calls to deep" (Ps. 42:2, 7). The depths of God's work in creation call to the depths of man's soul.

Surely all the majesty and marvel and miracle around us are
not a cosmic accident, the fortuitous concourse of atoms, the
products of happenstance. These vast and verifiable realities
of the universe are the work of a mighty and magnificent
Creator. As we ponder the depths of God's creation, the scin-
tillating stars hung out like silver lamps in the dark vastness,
the profuse thoroughfares of the stellar systems, we hear a
voice from the deep of creation speaking to the depths of our
being. We are assured that this is our Father's world.

> God of the galaxies, help me to ever have "the secret of see-
> ing." Enable me to look beyond the stars to the One who fash-
> ioned and holds them in His hands. And then let me thrill to
> the wonder of wonders, the Creator who holds my life in His
> mighty hands.

Portrait Sixty-two

THE MIRACLE OF RAIN

He wraps up the water in His clouds (Job 26:8).

Job won the debate with his accusers. He rebutted their lock-step tradition and prosperity theology. His faith and integrity emerged triumphant in trial. In this passage, he rose to lofty eloquence on the sovereignty and omnipotence of God the Creator. Bible expositor Andrew Blackwood writes of this discourse, "As it stands today, the song in all its wondrous beauty . . . is the most beautiful section in the book" (*Devotional Introduction to Job*, p. 208).

God's creative work is depicted by Job as *creatio ex nihilo*—creation out of nothing. Man can manufacture, make something out of raw material, but only God can create something out of nothing. Job stated, "He spreads out the northern skies over empty space, He suspends the earth over nothing" (26:7). The author of the Epistle to the Hebrews echoes that theme: "By faith we understand that the universe was formed at God's command, so that what is seen was not made out of what was visible" (Heb. 11:3).

Among the marvels of God's creation, Job cited the clouds that hold vast amounts of water yet do not rend apart under their load: "He wraps up the water in His clouds, yet the clouds do not burst under their weight." Clouds are one of nature's most common sights. We take them and their miracle for granted. Yet, our planet and all the life it hosts could not survive but for the life-giving rain they dispense.

Job would have marveled even more had he known what we have been taught about the marvel of God's escalator of evaporation that lifts moisture from the oceans and the earth. Then, carried by wind currents in clouds across continents, the moisture finally returns to the earth in the form of raindrops. The earth is spanked by its showers and gives forth its fecundity of growth and life. Man is refreshed and sustained by its life-giving liquid. Rain and water are among God's grand providences to humankind.

Job's faith in time of trial was strengthened by his affirmation of the sovereignty of God and His marvels of creation. Beyond the commonplace, Job saw the creative handiwork of God.

Sovereign God, with Job I stand amazed at the marvels of Your creation all about me. Strengthen and confirm my faith by an awareness of Your presence and power in the world of wonders around me.

Portrait Sixty-three

THE GARNISHED HEAVENS

By His Spirit He hath garnished the heavens (Job 26:13, KJV).

As Job continued his eulogy to the sovereignty of God, he presented one of the most striking and beautiful descriptions of God's creative work. Here we defer to the *Authorized (King James) Version*, which is peerless in its rendering of this verse: "By His Spirit He hath garnished the heavens." *Garnish* means to "adorn, embellish, decorate." God's creation is not only mighty, it is magnificent; it is not only awesome, it is adorned; it is not only great, it is glorious.

My favorite sight in nature is a star-bejeweled sky on a dark night. How tragic that many growing up in our urban culture never really see the majesty and beauty of the stars. Do you recall when first you were enraptured by God's garnished heavens?

One such moment is enshrined in our family archives of memory. It was on a camping trip in northern Canada. After the evening campfire had died down, we walked to the lakeside where there was an open view and gazed up at a sky festooned with stars. It was one of those clear, dark nights when the stars sparkle in resplendent glory. I'll never forget the spontaneous expression of one of our children, about seven years old at the time. He looked up at the dazzling sight of the star-studded sky and exclaimed in a reverent tone, "I never knew there were so many stars!" It was a moment of prized and precious discovery.

In these later years, at our personal mountain retreat, when our family is gathered on a summer evening, we sometimes go to the top of the mountain, taking with us our "star chairs"—chaise lounges that enable us to be horizontal, the only proper way to view a star-spangled sky. Then we just gaze at the dazzling spectacle staged by the Creator that fills the soul with awe and wonder.

The old couplet certainly applies to Job: "Two men looked through prison bars; One saw mud, the other saw stars." Job looked from his scars to God's stars and that made a difference. The Creator has gloriously garnished the heavens. God has written His autograph across the velvet scroll of the night sky with His stars which sparkle as jewels. The pageantry of the heavens eloquently proclaims His majesty and might.

God, who has endowed the world with beauty, touch my life with the radiance of Your love and the grace of Your peace that I may reflect Your beauty and glory.

Portrait Sixty-four
THE WHISPER OF HIM

How faint the whisper we hear of Him! (Job 26:14)

Job continued to rise to sublime poetic heights as he eulogized the greatness and government of God in creation. After citing some of the marvels of God's creation, he conceded:

And these are but the outer fringe of His works;
how faint the whisper we hear of Him!
Who then can understand the thunder of His power?
(26:14)

We are overcome with awe when we ponder the majesty and magnificence of God's creation. Yet Job reminds us that we see only the fringe of His works and hear only the faintest whisper of Him in contrast to the thunder of His power.

God is infinite and mortal capacity has its limits. The finite cannot comprehend the infinite. The human cannot understand the divine. Mortality cannot grasp the eternal. As an ant, incredibly as it is created, cannot enter into an understanding of humanity, so man cannot understand the infinite, the omniscient, the omnipotent, and the omnipresent God. Through the Prophet Isaiah, God reminds us:

"For My thoughts are not your thoughts,
neither are your ways My ways," declares the Lord.
"As the heavens are higher than the earth,

so are My ways higher than your ways
and My thoughts than your thoughts" (Isa. 55:8-9).

When assailed by troubles and trial, it is good to remember
that we do have an all-knowing, all-powerful, all-present, and
all-loving God. Though infinite, God is not unapproachable,
unknowable, aloof, or unconcerned about us and our needs.
The Incarnation and Calvary forever settled that question. The
Infinite stooped to become the Intimate in the miracle of the
manger. Divine love had its supreme articulation on the cross.
Our Creator is the God who condescended to make Himself
known and to draw us into an eternal and loving fellowship
with Him. The loving whisper (or was it God's thunder?) of
His sacrifice on Calvary has resonated around the world and
will ultimately climax in the grand Hallelujah Chorus of
heaven.

In his masterpiece "To a Waterfowl," William Cullen Bryant
describes the waterfowl pursuing its solitary way, guided by
an unseen Power "whose care teaches thy way along that
pathless coast." He concludes with an expression of confidence in the God who reveals the "outer fringe of His works"
in His care for His creatures:

Thou'rt gone, the abyss of heaven
Hath swallowed up Thy form; yet, on my heart
Deeply has sunk the lesson Thou has given,
And shalt not soon depart.

He, who from zone to zone,
Guides through the boundless sky thy certain flight,
In the long way that I must tread alone,
Will lead my steps aright.

*Great and Mighty God, I thank You also for the revelation
You give me in Your Word that "God is love."*

Portrait Sixty-five
A CONSCIENCE WITHOUT REPROACH

My conscience will not reproach me (Job 27:6).

"Every man has within a Guardian Angel," states one anonymous writer, "for conscience is ever on the watch, ever ready to warn us of danger." Another, under the same pseudonym, writes, "Conscience is condensed character." Self-interest asks, "Is it gratifying?" Expediency asks, "Is it advantageous?" Caution asks, "Is it safe?" But conscience asks, "Is it right?"

Conscience is one of the great gifts of God to man. It is a moral compass to keep us in the right direction. It is a divine voice in our soul. It is, in the words of Robert Browning: "The great beacon light God sets in all." Defined by William Cowper, it is "the still, small voice." Lord Byron also pays his poetic tribute:

> Whatever creed be taught or land be trod,
> Man's conscience is the oracle of God.

Job's integrity was assailed by his contenders. They vigorously asserted that Job's calamities were the consequences of sin. But Job asserted his integrity, declaring: "I will maintain my righteousness and never let go of it; my conscience will not reproach me as long as I live" (27:6). Because he had a conscience without reproach, his faith stood firm under its fierce testing.

Sometimes a person may feel he is suffering because of sin he has committed. A sense of guilt may overwhelm him and make him say, "This has happened to me because of my sin." There are three ways to resolve such a problem. First, realize that suffering, in general, is neutral. All persons, good and evil, sinners and saints, are vulnerable to the afflictions of life. Second, and best, is like Job—to have a conscience without reproach. Third, if there has been sin, confess it, repent of it, and accept God's forgiveness.

An anonymous sage speaks to Job's experience: "A bad conscience embitters the sweetest comforts; a good one sweetens the bitterest crosses." Because Job was blameless before God, he could stand tall when the winds of adversity beat savagely on him. So too, in the day of our testing, it will be our integrity that will enable faith to withstand the storms.

Let us be able to say with the Apostle Paul, "So I strive always to keep my conscience clear before God and man" (Acts 24:16).

Holy Spirit, keep me responsive to the divine still, small voice planted within my soul.

Portrait Sixty-six

THE TREASURE OF WISDOM

But where can wisdom be found? (Job 28:12)

Our poet-author describes in graphic terms man's mining for treasures buried deep in the earth. Scientist Jastro calls this chapter "one of the most impressive bits of literature in the entire Old Testament." "He searches the farthest recesses" for silver, gold and precious gems. As man tunnels the earth:

> Sapphires come from its rocks,
> and its dust contains nuggets of gold.
> No bird of prey knows that hidden path,
> no falcon's eye has seen it. . . .
> He tunnels through the rock;
> His eyes see all its treasures.
> He searches the sources of the rivers
> and brings hidden things to light (28:6-11).

After describing how man's most diligent effort is required to find earth's hidden treasures, he gives us his bottom line: "But where can wisdom be found?" (28:12) It is posed, of course, as a rhetorical question. Wisdom, a greater treasure than all the precious metals and jewels of earth, is inaccessible. No Herculean effort, no technology known to man can find wisdom. Man's ingenuity is marvelous, but it cannot discover wisdom—it is not to be found in the land of the living (28:13), nor in the depth of the sea (28:14), nor can it be bought—it is beyond price (28:15-19).

But Job gave the answer to man's search for wisdom—"God understands the way to it and He alone knows where it dwells" (28:23). This chapter ends with Job's one-sentence summary on wisdom: "The fear of the Lord—that is wisdom, and to shun evil is understanding" (28:28). Centuries later, Milton gave us a paraphrase of this insight: "The end of all learning is to know God and out of that knowledge to love and serve Him."

Wisdom comes from God. Every time we open our Bible, it speaks to us. When we commune with God in prayer, we hear its accents. When we see a godly life, we encounter its eloquence. When we worship, its whispered secrets fall on our ears.

If men will search so arduously for the lesser treasures of earth, how much more should we be willing to expend ourselves to be enriched with the largesse of God's wisdom. It too is a hard-won treasure. It requires a passionate longing for what God has for us. We must diligently explore and ferret out the riches of prayer, of God's Word, of worship and praise, and then we will discover the priceless treasure of wisdom from God.

A.W. Tozer reminds us of the cost of wisdom: "Let a man become enamored of Eternal Wisdom and set his heart to win her and he takes on himself a full-time, all-engaging pursuit. . . . Thereafter his whole life will be filled with seekings and findings, self-repudiations, tough disciplines and daily dyings as he is being crucified unto the world and the world unto him" (*A Treasury of A.W. Tozer*, Baker Book House, 1980, p. 151).

Let us also remember that Job gained his greatest wisdom in the school of affliction. Malcolm Muggeridge shares this remarkable testimony in *A Twentieth Century Testimony*: "Indeed I can say with complete truthfulness that everything I have learned in my seventy-five years in this world, everything that has truly enhanced and enlightened my existence, has been through affliction and not through happiness." It is in the deepest recesses of life's journeyings that we find God's priceless treasures.

God of wisdom, forgive my foolish ways. Lead me each day to the source of all wisdom, the One "in whom are hidden all the treasures of wisdom and knowledge."

Portrait Sixty-seven

REMEMBERING HAPPIER THINGS

How I long for the months gone by (Job 29:2).

In "Locksley Hall," Tennyson comments on Job's experience in the twenty-ninth chapter: "Truth the poet sings/That a sorrow's crown of sorrow/Is remembering happier things." Job, continuing in his final discourse with his contestants, took a long retrospective glance of his past happiness. His reflection evoked fame, family life, felicity, prosperity, prestige, power, opulence, esteem. He reminisced sadly:

> How I long for the months gone by. . . .
> Oh, for the days when I was in my prime,
> when God's intimate friendship blessed my house . . .
> and my children were around me. . . .
> I dwelt as a king among his troops (29:2, 4-5, 25).

It is easy for human nature to think sadly, rather than appreciatively, on past days of good and glory. A man whose son died at twenty-one was not able to overcome his grief and mourning. One day he was asked by his minister, "If the choice had been offered you of having him twenty-one years or not at all, which would you have chosen?" The joy of happy, sunlit hours need not always be overshadowed by the storm clouds that have come.

Corrie ten Boom is a saint of our time who endured brutality and tragedy in the Nazi war camp because she dared to make her home a haven for the Jews. She is one of Job's modern counterparts. She knew what it meant to lose everything. She lost her home, beloved family, precious possessions, status, and security. She says from that experience she had learned "to hold everything loosely." She discovered in her years of walking with her Lord that when she grasped things tightly, it would hurt when the Lord would have to pry her fingers loose. For each disciple today, it is one of the deeper disciplines of life.

Dear Lord, help me not to let the shadows of the present dim or obscure the sunlight of the past. Help me not to live this day regretfully but joyfully.

Portrait Sixty-eight
CHAMPION OF THE POOR

I was a father to the needy (Job 29:16).

In his prime, Job was a champion of the poor. He reminisced:

> Whoever heard of me spoke well of me,
> and those who saw me commended me,
> because I rescued the poor who cried for help,
> and the fatherless who had none to assist him.
> The man who was dying blessed me;
> I made the widow's heart sing.
> I put on righteousness as my clothing;
> justice was my robe and my turban.
> I was eyes to the blind
> and feet to the lame.
> I was a father to the needy;
> I took up the case of the stranger.
> I broke the fangs of the wicked
> and snatched the victims from their teeth (29:11-17).

What an example today for the people of God! There is a danger of which the Christian must beware. It does not appear in any of the works of theology. But let's give it a name—"spiritual segregation." Its symptom is that of the spiritual life relegated to prescribed places, times, and exercises. It forces a dichotomy between the sacred and non-sacred. The sacred is slow to wed the secular for fear that they will be incompatible.

It results in the life becoming spiritually anemic. It makes my religion a minimal factor instead of a maximum force. Faith becomes compartmentalized rather than integrated into all of life. It leaves untouched some of the most vital areas of relationships and responsibilities. It ignores the hurts and crises of my brother in the world who needs my love and action.

Commissioner Andrew S. Miller, as national commander of The Salvation Army, has stated on behalf of his organization that when its human services work is done right, one cannot tell the difference between the spiritual and social work of the movement. He states that they are blended with a harmony that knows no distinction between our faith and compassionate response to the needs of others.

May believers today be eyes to the blind, feet to the lame, fathers to the needy, friends to the stranger. God calls us to be His servants in a troubled and tortured world.

God of love, help me to be willing to pay the price of caring in a world where so many are weary and wounded.

MAN'S EXTREMITY—
GOD'S OPPORTUNITY

But now (Job 30:1).

Job's world had gone topsy-turvy on him; it had turned around completely. After recalling his magnificent past, he now mourned his miserable present. "But now" was his plaintive cry that echoes across the centuries.

Job 30 is Job's requiem of regret. Job had gone from popularity to ridicule—"They mock me. . . . I have become a byword among them. They detest me and keep their distance" (30:1, 9-10).

Job lamented his regression from strength to weakness. In a striking metaphor he complained, "God has unstrung my bow" (30:11). The archer's bow in that day was the primary weapon for hunting and warfare, the symbol of power. In graphic language, he described himself as under siege (30:12-14), falling from dignity to disgrace, bemoaning "my dignity is driven away as by the wind" (30:15).

In his requiem of regret, he cried, "Terrors overwhelm me. . . . My life ebbs away. . . . I am reduced to dust and ashes. . . . The churning inside me never stops. . . . My harp is tuned to mourning, and my flute to the sound of wailing" (30:15-16, 19, 27, 31).

Well, what do we do when life comes tumbling down? What do we do when we come to the end of our rope? Hang on? But how?

Charles Colson testifies: "Sure, Watergate caused my world

to crash around me and sent me to prison. I lost many of the mainstays of my existence—the awards, the six-figure income and lifestyle to match, arguing cases in the highest courts, a position of power at the right hand of the President of the United States. But only when I lost them did I find a far greater gain: knowing Christ. . . . I wouldn't trade the toughest day of the last few years—which includes those in prison—for the best day of the forty years before. . . . What I couldn't find in my quest for power and success—that is, true security and meaning—I discovered in prison where all worldly props had been stripped away" (*Who Speaks for God?* Crossway Books, 1985, pp. 47, 181).

The Chinese combine two characters for the word *crisis*. One character means "danger" and the other "opportunity." These two possibilities are inherent in every crisis. A crisis is a crossroads, and the outcome is determined by which path is taken. When a person is described as "critical" in medical terms it means he can move either toward life or death. Just so, the crises of life present not only danger but also opportunity.

Our extremity is God's opportunity.

Help me, Lord, to be as the man who built his house on solid rock, so when the storms beat on me, I will stand firm.

Portrait Seventy
DAYS OF SUFFERING

Days of suffering confront me (Job 30:27).

The Book of Job is about suffering. It is the world's greatest textbook on human trial and tragedy. Thus Job's statement, "Days of suffering confront me" is generic to this book. It is a summary of Job's experience throughout most of this account.

So many people respond to the Book of Job because they too have passed through suffering and trial. They identify with the one who went through great calamities and who hurled his question at God: "Why?" Job's trademark of suffering gives him a universal standing among mankind. Who of us has not been constrained to say at some time or another, "Days of suffering confront me"?

Rabbi Harold Kushner shares a trenchant insight in his bestseller, *When Bad Things Happen to Good People* (Avon): "No one ever promised us a life free from pain and disappointment. The most anyone promised us was that we would not be alone in our pain, and that we would be able to draw upon a source outside ourselves for the strength and courage we would need to survive life's tragedies and life's unfairness. . . . We can redeem these tragedies from senselessness by imposing meaning on them. . . . The question we should be asking is . . . 'Now that this has happened to me, what am I going to do about it?' Not, 'Where does the tragedy come from?' but 'Where does it lead?' "

We are not alone in our suffering and trial. We have a

Resource, One who cares and comforts and enables us to find blessing even in brokenness. Lucy Booth-Helberg reminds us of this truth in song:

When you feel weakest, dangers surround,
Subtle temptations, troubles abound,
Nothing seems hopeful, nothing seems glad,
All is despairing, everything sad;

Keep on believing, Jesus is near;
Keep on believing, there's nothing to fear;
Keep on believing, this is the way;
Faith in the night as well as the day.

If all were easy, if all were bright,
Where would the cross be, and where the fight?
But in the hardness, God gives to you
Chances of proving that you are true.

Our Father, we know You have not promised to surround us with immunity from the ills to which the flesh is heir. But we pray that when they come we will be found adequate through Your grace.

Portrait Seventy-one

WHEN HEALTH FAILS

My body burns with fever (Job 30:30).

Some souls seem destined to enter the dim cathedral of pain. Some endure as their lot a life of physical affliction and handicap. Job experienced the limits of physical suffering. He knew what it was to be deprived of rest and sleep: "Night pierces my bones; my gnawing pains never rest" (30:17). His very skin became charred and peeling—"My skin grows black and peels"—and he cried out, "My body burns with fever" (30:30).

Some who read this book will identify with Job's physical suffering, if not for themselves then perhaps for a loved one. The loss of health can be a heavy cross to carry, a lonely burden to be borne, a traumatic and life-changing experience.

But how assuring to read the glowing biographies of people who found God's surprises in their suffering, His presence in their pain, His assurance in their affliction, and His strength for their struggle. One radiant example is that of Mrs. Charles Cowman who, with her beloved husband, served a number of years as a missionary in the Orient. Her radiant testimony is an encouragement to any who go through the dark night of suffering:

> We were afar in the mountain fastnesses of Japan, engaged in evangelistic work, when one evening, like a bolt out of the blue, came the stroke that completely changed everything in our lives. A doctor was summoned hastily, and after a hurried examination he said to me, "Your husband's work is

finished. Take him to the homeland immediately, if you would not bury him in foreign soil." "Worn out" was the term that the physician used. We boarded a steamer and put out to sea. What lay ahead of us? We could only trust and wait. . . . What a change for this keen, active man! From the din of the battle to the seclusion of the sick chamber. From the glow and glory of the work he loved so dearly, to the utter abandonment of it all. . . . A triumphant faith was needed just when God gave it, and he found that it was possible to praise God in the darkest hour that ever swept a human life. It was my privilege to be by his side through the six long, pain-filled years. . . . One day, when lonely and bereft, a sweet voice whispered to me, "Pass on to other troubled hearts some of the messages that were helpful to you throughout the years of testing." So a book was compiled, and the first edition of *Streams in the Desert* was sent on its errand of love (Mrs. Charles Cowman, *Mountain Trailways*, Rand McNally, 1947, pp. 309-311).

The rest is history in the annals of Christian publications. *Streams in the Desert* became a devotional classic. Its radiant meditations have gone throughout the world in its over thirty editions. And it all emerged from an experience of pain and suffering. How marvelously God's grace comes to us in our hour of need. For each of us, when we trust Him, He will turn our pain into gain and our tears into pearls.

Our health can be snatched from us in a moment of time—an accident, a heart attack or stroke, the onslaught of disease. But in the life of a Christian, there abides God's love and care and sustaining presence.

Mrs. Cowman has shared her secret with her readers:

Measure thy life by loss and not gain;
not by the wine drunk but the wine poured forth;
For love's strength standeth in love's sacrifice,
And he who suffers most has most to give.

God of grace, through Your comfort make me a comforter, and through Your grace make me a blessing to those who carry a heavy cross.

Portrait Seventy-two
THE EXAMINED LIFE

If my steps have turned from the path (Job 31:7).

It has been stated that the most famous poem of the English language is Rudyard Kipling's "If." Eleven times in that delightful poem Kipling sounds his watchword, "if." His opening lines could well apply to Job:

> If you can keep your head when all about you
>   Are losing theirs and blaming it on you,
> If you can trust yourself when all men doubt you,
>   But make allowance for their doubting too . . .

Job gave us his "if" poem in the thirty-first chapter of his book. These were his final words in the great debate and are a disavowal of his guilt. He examined himself with nineteen hypotheses, each beginning with "if." It is a catalog of sins that lends itself for our self-examination.

It is good, on occasion, to stand back and take inventory of our spiritual life. Plato, writing in the fourth century B.C., said, "The life which is unexamined is not worth living." The psalmist prayed, "Examine my heart and my mind" (Ps. 26:2). The Apostle Paul urged believers to "examine yourselves to see whether you are in the faith; test yourselves" (2 Cor. 13:5). Job, accused of sin by his peers, put himself through this rigorous test to prove his integrity before God and man.

Job's blameless character, as attested by God in the opening of this book, was further confirmed by this test of his integrity. How many people could stand under the scrutiny of these specific questions that cover such a broad range of responsibility before God and others? This chapter reveals why Job was singled out by God as a sterling example of the righteous person.

Job did not test himself by the popular standards or theology of his day. His standards were not shaped by the majority but by God. Thomas Kelly in his classic, *A Testament of Devotion*, points out, "No average goodness will do, measuring of our lives by our fellows, but only a relentless, inexorable divine standard. No relatives suffice; only absolutes satisfy the soul committed to holy obedience."

When we examine our own lives, what is our standard? What are the criteria by which we can test our faith and practice? Dietrich Bonhoeffer, writing from a Nazi prison cell, addressed this subject with profound insight: "Who stands fast? Only the man whose final standard is not his reason, his principles, his conscience, his freedom, or his virtue, but who is ready to sacrifice all this when he is called to obedient and responsible action in faith and in exclusive allegiance to God— the responsible man, who tries to make his whole life an answer to the question and call of God" (*Letters and Papers from Prison*, p. 5).

When we ask God to examine our lives, we must come with openness and honesty. From Him we cannot hide our sin and failure. We appear before Him, not as we are seen by others, but as we really are, questing and struggling to be what He wants us to be. With His revelation will come forgiveness for our sin and enablement to go on from strength to strength.

> *With the psalmist I pray, "Search me, O God, and know my heart; test me and know my anxious thoughts. See if there is any offensive way in me, and lead me in the way everlasting"* (Ps. 139:23-24).

Portrait Seventy-three

THE TEST OF HONESTY

If I have walked in falsehood (Job 31:5).

The bravest moment of a man's life is when he takes an objective look at himself. Job relentlessly reviewed the moral issues that comprised his avowal of innocence.

"If I have walked in falsehood" is an acid test to apply to oneself. What question can be more probing than "Am I truthful?" "Are there any conditions under which I would tell a lie?" "Can I be depended on to tell the truth no matter what the cost?"

How easy it is to be less than truthful, even for religious people. There are subtle as well as salient perversions of truth, such as in the following sampling:

exaggerations to make an impression;
twisting the truth in an appeal for funds;
taking credit for what we have not earned;
submitting inaccurate financial records;
misrepresenting goods for sale;
false excuses for absence, lateness or duties undone;
cheating on an exam.

Have I been truthful with other people's reputations or disparaged them to make myself look better? Have I been free from rationalization, justifying an otherwise discreditable action? Have I been truthful with myself? With God? Christian psychologist James R. Dolby writes: "Most of our lives have been spent learning to play the game of deception. . . . We are

159

caught in a pattern of dishonesty . . . to be honest with our-selves is not natural" (*I, Too, Am Man*, Word, 1969, p. 1).

Winston Churchill said, "Every now and then a man will stumble upon truth, and usually he picks himself up and goes on again." It can be painfully difficult to confront truth. Usu-ally truth lags behind, limping along on the arm of time. Sir Isaac Newton was thrown in jail as an old man for insisting on the theory of the law of gravity. The man who invented the telephone (not Alexander Graham Bell) was thrown in jail for twenty years for his "heresy" that man could talk over wire. It requires openness and courage to confront truth.

May we so live truthfully that, as Job of old, we can have Him "weigh me in honest scales and He will know that I am blameless" (31:6).

> *Christ the Truth, save me from self-deception and the subtle duplicities of life. Help me to be open, honest, and truthful with myself, with You, and with others.*

Portrait Seventy-four

THE GIANT, LUST

If my heart has been enticed by a woman (Job 31:9).

Job had much to say about lust in his test for integrity. At the outset, he gave to us the secret of victory over lust. It is a decision and dedication, even before any temptation may assail, to avoid impure thoughts and lustful enticements. His soliloquy opened: "I made a covenant with my eyes not to look lustfully at a girl." How many would have been saved from disaster if they had done as Job?

Job vowed: "If my heart has been enticed by a woman, or if I have lurked at my neighbor's door," and then warned that the sin of lust is "a fire that burns to destruction" (31:9, 12).

The Book of Proverbs solemnly reminds us, "Many are the victims she has brought down; her slain are a mighty throng" (Prov. 7:26). Could that writer have been remembering Samson, who is described by Charles Swindoll as "a he-man with a she-weakness"? Swindoll further details Samson's demise to lust: "Once the pride of Israel became a clown of the Philistines. The perfumed memories of erotic pleasure in Gaza are now overwhelmed by the putrid stench of a Philistine dungeon. Chalk up another victim for lust." Or perhaps the writer of Proverbs was remembering "the giant which slew David."

Have we not all known strong men who have fallen prey to the lure of lust? What victims it has claimed in all ages. Let us, as Job, make a covenant with our eyes and our bodies and, by the power of the Holy Spirit, keep ourselves pure. It was Sir Galahad who said, "I have the strength of ten men because my heart is pure." A pure heart and life will make us strong and stalwart for God.

Lord of purity, with the verse writer I would pray, "Purge the dark halls of thought, Here let Thy will be wrought, Each wish and feeling brought, captive to Thee."

Portrait Seventy-five

A SOCIAL CONSCIENCE

If I have denied the desires of the poor (Job 31:16).

"A conversion is incomplete if it does not leave a man with an intense social consciousness," writes William Barclay, "if it does not fill him with a sense of overwhelming responsibility for the world." Job had an acute social conscience. We find throughout the book a number of references to his response to those in need around him. Here again he maintained that he was responsive to the needy:

> If I have denied the desires of the poor
>   or let the eyes of the widow grow weary,
> If I have kept my bread to myself,
>   not sharing it with the fatherless . . .
> If I· have seen anyone perishing for lack of clothing,
>   or a needy man without a garment,
> and his heart did not bless me
>   for warming him with the fleece from my sheep (31:16-20).

The church must never become an island of believers isolated from the cries and hurts of our world. The world will shrug its shoulders and walk away if they see us as pious people, connoisseurs of preaching and praise, but uninvolved and uncaring for the multitudes in danger and destitution.

Our Lord's Parable on The Good Samaritan should be a rapier thrust that forever deals a deathblow to such a narrow concept.

The religious leaders in the parable may have had urgent "sacred" business that would not allow time for such a secular distraction as helping the wounded man on the Jericho Road. The lesson of our Lord's parable is always contemporary. It is ever a mandate for Christianity in action, out where the air is blowing, where the issues are real, where people are hurting.

Colonel Giles C. Barrett of The Salvation Army articulated its motto, "Heart To God and Hand To Man," as a mission to the trapped, the troubled, the transgressor, the shut-in, the shut-out, the sick; a parent to the young, a partner to the aged, a participant in the community, and a pastor to the flock. Evangelism and practical ministry are obverse and reverse sides of the coin that makes up the over 100-year thrust of the movement that has been a social conscience to the church at large. It has sought to serve at the front lines of human need with the Bible in one hand and a cup of cold water in the other. William Booth and his successive generations of warriors have an affinity with the philosophy of famed missionary C.T. Studd:

> Some wish to live within the sound
>   Of church or chapel bell,
> I want to run a rescue shop
>   Within a yard of hell.

We as individuals may not be ready for that much of a commitment, but may we be sensitive and responsive to the people around us and in the world who need our caring and sharing.

Loving Father, I would pray, as Bill Pierce lived and prayed, "Let my heart be broken by the things that break the heart of God."

Portrait Seventy-six
TRUST IN GOLD

If I have put my trust in gold (Job 31:24).

Job, of all people of his day, could well have put his trust in his fabulous wealth. He was the richest man in the East. There were many in his day who worshiped idols made of gold. But his integrity was above such false security:

> If I have put my trust in gold
>   or said to pure gold, "You are my security,"
> If I have rejoiced over my great wealth,
>   the fortune my hand had gained . . .
> I would have been unfaithful to God on high (31:24-28).

Many in our society today seem possessed by their possessions. "Contemporary culture is plagued by the passion to possess," writes Richard Foster in *Freedom of Simplicity* (Harper & Row). Foster's insightful writing disturbs our comfort and cultural pattern as he trenchantly declares: "The lust for affluence in contemporary society has become psychotic. Christian simplicity frees us from this modern mania. It brings sanity to our compulsive extravagance, and peace to our frantic spirit. . . . People once again become more important than possessions."

The story is told of a simple-living Quaker who was sitting on his porch while his new neighbor moved in. He watched with interest as the newcomer unloaded his goods. Every kind of trinket and expensive gadget imaginable seemed to come off the moving trucks. The Quaker was unaffected by the new family's collection. Finally, he strolled over to greet the folks. After an exchange of chitchat, the Quaker turned to leave. Looking at the piles of fancy belongings, he said with a stroke of wit, "If, neighbor, thou dost ever need anything, come to see me and I will tell thee how to get along without it."

Perhaps we all need a lesson in how to get along without some of the accretions that we think necessary. G.K. Chesterton wittily reminds us that there are two ways to get enough: one is to continue to accumulate more and more. The other is to desire less.

With Job, let us not put our trust in material things, but in those things which are eternal. Our security is not in our portfolios but in God's promises.

> Dear Lord, help me to heed Your Word to not store up the transient treasures of earth but to store up treasures in heaven that will endure for all eternity.

Portrait Seventy-seven
PLIGHT OF THE HOMELESS

No stranger had to spend the night in the street (Job 31:32).

In Job's day, hospitality was vital for travelers who made long, slow journeys with no rows of motels or Holiday Inns awaiting them. Sometimes the alternative to hospitality would be to spend the night outdoors. Job included in his defense of his integrity, "But no stranger had to spend the night in the street, for my door was always open to the traveler" (30:32).

Today, in the affluent U.S., we are confronted with the domestic crisis of many who have to spend the night in the street. The homeless population is estimated to be as high as 3 million. The demographics of the homeless have changed dramatically. Their ranks have become swollen with females and families. The crisis is exacerbated by the lack of affordable housing and the deinstitutionalization of the mentally ill from long-term custodial care.

Job's feeding the hungry and housing the stranger was to have ultimate endorsement and mandate from our Lord in His unforgettable words: "I was hungry and you gave Me something to eat, I was thirsty and you gave Me something to drink, I was a stranger and you invited Me in" (Matt. 25:35).

Colonel John Gowans of The Salvation Army has given us a haunting poem, *The Homeless*, that ends with the challenge:

I care! says Christ. I know what "homeless" means.
I'm with the hungry in the line for beans!

I know the pitted pavement of the street,
And skid row bears the imprint of My feet.
I've often had no place to lay My head.
At Bethlehem they borrowed Me a bed!

You want to find Me? Then you'd better come
And face the stinking of the city slum,
Where men live daily wishing they were dead
And give away their dignity for bread.

. . . And grasp this truth, for it could set you free:
All that you do for them, you do for Me.

Help me, Lord, to find You among the least, the lowest, and the lost to whom You would have me be a channel of Your compassion.

Portrait Seventy-eight
SECRET SINS

If I have concealed my sin (Job 31:33).

At the time of this writing, a rash of "secret sins" have come to light, or rather, to the spotlight. A top-running presidential candidate dropped out of the primary race following the press reports on his "womanizing" and an admission of adultery. Members of our elite Marine Corps were found guilty of trading top U.S. secrets for sex in Moscow. A governor faces impeachment proceedings for fiscal improprieties. The world press has had a field day with the scandals of televangelists. We can all add our postscripts of those whom we have known whose secret sins suddenly came to light and the consequences that ensued. Acts committed in secret when revealed have had devastating impacts on their lives.

The Bible warns us, "You may be sure that your sin will find you out" (Num. 32:23). The psalmist prayed, "Cleanse Thou me from secret faults" (Ps. 19:12, KJV). In a deeper sense, however, there is no such thing as "secret sins." Our sins may not be known to others, but they are known to us. Most important, they are known to God. Our Lord taught us that "there is nothing concealed that will not be disclosed, or hidden that will not be made known" (Matt. 10:26).

We only fool ourselves if we think we can get away with sin. Sooner or later it will come to light. In the meantime, its consequences become registered in our hearts and souls. It robs us of God's presence and power. It compromises our witness. It stains our conscience. It hinders our devotional life. It deprives us of the peace of God. Even when not known to others, it will subtly manifest itself in the mirror of our soul.

Job, in his test for integrity, did not exempt himself from this probing and essential questioning. He stated, "If I have concealed my sin as men do, by hiding my guilt in my heart" (31:33). He was able to include in his vow of innocence that he harbored no concealed sin in his life, again corresponding to God's own commendation of him as a blameless man (1:8; 2:3).

In this series of examinations, of which we have considered only a few, Job cleared himself of any sinful deed or intention. He now rests his defense, and the chapter concludes with, "The words of Job are ended" (31:40).

Let us take a page from Job's spiritual diary and be sure we can stand before God and others with no concealed sin. To conceal sin is a no-win situation. Augustine reminds us that the consequence of sin is sin. Let us go on to full victory.

Heavenly Father, with the poet, Leslie Taylor-Hunt, I pray:

> *All my best works are naught,*
>   *Please they not Thee;*
> *Far past my busy hands*
>   *Thine eye doth see*
> *Into the depths of mind,*
> *Searching the plan designed,*
> *Gladdened when Thou dost find*
>   *First of all, Thee.*

Portrait Seventy-nine

AN ANGRY YOUNG MAN

Elihu . . . became very angry (Job 32:2).

Enter Elihu, the fourth friend, who has been standing on the sidelines, impatiently waiting to make himself heard. As a parenthesis, he appeared and disappeared, without reference in either the prologue or epilogue. He left a record of four poetic monologues (Job 32–37).

He ostentatiously presented himself, telling Job the wonderful things he would say. As Andrew Blackwood describes him, "One gathers that the speaker does not suffer from a surplus of modesty." His six-chapter, 165-verse speech is the longest in the book, confirming his statement, "I am full of words" (32:18). "Be silent," he told Job, "and I will teach you wisdom" (33:33).

He was an angry young man. Three times in the opening paragraph, Elihu was described as being angry. He was angry with Job (32:2), with the three friends (32:3), and because Job had bested his contestants (32:5). The case for tradition had been lost. Like some speakers we all have heard, "Words failed them" (32:15). But Elihu had no inhibitions. His impetuosity could no longer be restrained.

He is identified as "young in years" (32:6) and anger is often associated with youth. Experience and maturity have a way of tempering our impatience. "Rid yourselves of . . . anger," Paul urged believers (Col. 3:8). Seneca called anger "a brief insanity." Anger blasts the flower of friendship, ruptures relationships, destroys peace in the home, and incites crime and violence.

In Leningrad is a magnificent equestrian statue of Peter the Great with his hand uplifted, pointing his nation onward and eastward toward the sea. Peter was the maker of modern Russia and in many respects well deserves the name "great." But he was subject to maniacal outbursts of fury and anger, in one of which he killed his own son. Toward the end of his reign, Peter the Great remarked, "I have conquered an empire, but I was not able to conquer myself." In the Book of Proverbs we are told, "He that ruleth his spirit [is greater] than he that taketh a city" (Prov. 16:32, KJV). It is still true that the greatest conquest is self-conquest; the greatest control is self-control.

But Elihu felt constrained to speak out in defense of his theology and tradition. Though we today know his outlook was flawed, we are reminded that there is a time for anger to be vented. There is a time to be good and mad! Thomas Fuller described anger as "one of the sinews of the soul." God has given us a temper for a reason. Jesus Himself showed blazing anger as with whitened knuckles cracking the whip He drove the money changers out of the sacred precincts of the temple.

But anger must be properly motivated. Too often it is rooted in selfishness. Our Lord never showed anger on behalf of Himself, even when He was brutally pinioned to a cross.

We need to beware lest we commit the sin of not being angry in the face of injustice and man's inhumanity to man and the profaning of the sacred. Christians today should be good and mad over the 1½ million unborn babies aborted each year in the U.S., over the scourge of pornography that has become epidemic across the country, over the violence and sexploitation that invades our living rooms through television.

Let our anger not be as Elihu's pompous words, but as a conviction of the soul channeled into remedial action.

Christ of the whip and flashing eye, grant to me Your indignations when confronted with injustice, inhumanity, and profaning of the sacred.

Portrait Eighty
SONGS IN THE NIGHT

God . . . gives songs in the night (Job 35:10).

Stately passages of the book are often set on the lips of Job's accusers. In his long oration, Elihu left us some precious promises and textual jewels. He delivered the radiant statement "God . . . gives songs in the night."

Job knew well this beautiful providence of God. When the black curtain of catastrophe fell over his soul, he sang, "The Lord gave and the Lord has taken away; may the name of the Lord be praised" (1:21).

In his darkest hour, he gave the centuries the celebrated song, "I know that my Redeemer lives" (19:25). Think of it! From his pit of futility, Job rose to the pinnacle of faith with one of the most sublime songs of the Bible. His staunch affirmation has been translated classically into the stirring soprano strains of Handel's *Messiah*: "I Know That My Redeemer Liveth."

Think of it! Job's song in the night, given him by God, has sung its way through the centuries into our living rooms and hearts as we thrill to it anew each Advent and Easter season.

Think of it! From the Old Testament book of deepest darkness has come the song of the most radiant light. From the depths of gloom is given the song that lifts to the heights of glory. From the Old Testament's greatest tragedy, God brings the song of grand triumph!

It is just like God. What a powerful message this is for our testings and trials of life. Indeed, "In vain does Satan then oppose, For God is stronger than His foes!"

Thank You, God, that in our darkest night You give the light and the lift of a song. Help me to hear its majestic music.

Portrait Eighty-one

FROM A DARKENED ROOM

God . . . gives songs in the night (Job 35:10).

We have reflected on the sublime songs God gave to Job in his dark night of the soul. Many of our hymns were born in the crucible of life's trials. An anonymous poet has written:

Many a rapturous minstrel
  Among the sons of light,
Will say of his sweetest music,
  "I learned it in the night."
And many a rolling anthem
  That fills the Father's throne,
Sobbed out its first rehearsal
  In the shade of a darkened room.

Fanny Crosby's hymns have strengthened and nurtured millions of believers around the world. She was incredibly prolific, composing over 6,000 hymns, with some 3,000 of them published. How enriched has been our singing and experience with such standards as "Blessed Assurance," "Jesus, Keep Me Near the Cross," "Tell Me the Story of Jesus," and "To God Be the Glory." Fanny Crosby did her composing in a dark room. Total darkness—for she was blind. But God lit a light in her mind and soul that enabled her to see and share "rivers of pleasure" and "visions of rapture." God gave her songs that will shine on through eternity.

Joseph Scriven wrote twenty-four lines to comfort his mother during a time of serious illness when he could not go to her. He sent his poem with the prayer that it would remind her of her never-failing Friend. The poem was later put to music, and we know it today as "What a Friend We Have in Jesus." God gave him a comforting song in the night.

One of our most inspiring hymns is George Matheson's "O Love that will not let me go." Its second verse reads:

> O Light that followest all my way,
> I yield my flickering torch to Thee;
> My heart restores its borrowed ray,
> That in Thy sunshine's blaze its day
> May brighter, fairer be.

Matheson, a blind preacher, says of his composition, "This hymn was the fruit of a mental suffering. The lyric came to me spontaneously without conscious effort." God gave him a radiant song in the night.

Are you going through your own dark night of the soul? If so, listen carefully and prayerfully. God has a special song for you.

Thank You, God, that as the song reminds us, "There is never a day so dreary, there is never a night so long, but the soul that is trusting Jesus will somewhere find a song."

Portrait Eighty-two
SORROWS INTO SYMPHONIES

God . . . gives songs in the night (Job 35:10).

Job was a forerunner of the great company to whom God would give songs in the night. So many of our favorite hymns were composed in night seasons of the soul.

Charlotte Elliott wrote "Just As I Am" as a helpless invalid. Frances Ridley Havergal, who penned "Take My Life," suffered chronic ill health. Out of the horrors of the Thirty Years' War, during which he conducted as many as forty funerals a day and a total of over 4,000 during his ministry, Pastor Martin Rinkart wrote the song of thanksgiving, "Now Thank We All Our God."

William Cowper knew what it was like to have sunlight and hope eclipsed by despair. He tried to end it all one bleak morning by swallowing poison. His suicide attempt failed. He then went to the Thames River, intending to hurl himself over the bridge, and was "strangely restrained." The next morning he fell on a sharp knife—and broke the blade. Failing in these attempts, he tried to hang himself but was found, taken down unconscious, and revived. Later he picked up a Bible and began to read the Book of Romans. It was then Cowper finally met the God of the storms and night seasons, submitting to the One who had pursued him through so many desolate days and dreary nights. From out of the whirlwinds of his experiences, he sat down and recorded with these familiar words his summary of the Lord's dealing: "God moves in a mysterious way His wonders to perform; He plants His footsteps in the sea, and rides upon the storm."

Amy Carmichael, missionary extraordinary to India, from her bed in constant pain, ministered through her devotional writings and poetry. Through the power of the Holy Spirit, we will be able to sing her victorious words:

> Before the winds that blow do cease,
> Teach me to dwell within Thy calm;
> Before the pain has passed in peace,
> Give me, my God, to sing a psalm.
> Let me not lose the chance to prove
> The fullness of enabling love.

Heavenly Father, when the shadows come and the storm is loud, help me to hear and learn to sing the song that You give in the night season.

A SONG IN THE STORM

God . . . gives songs in the night (Job 35:10).

Because this text of Job is so rich with human experience and contemporary application, let us take one more dramatic example of a song that came in the night.

After the great Chicago fire of 1871, Mr. Spafford, a Chicago lawyer, arranged an ocean voyage for his family to Europe, where he would join them later. The ship on which the happy family sailed, the *Ville du Havre*, never got farther than half-way across the Atlantic. In the dead of the night, it was rammed by a sailing vessel and cut in two. In the confusion and disaster that followed, Mrs. Spafford saw all four of her daughters swept away to their deaths. A falling mast knocked her unconscious, and a wave freakishly deposited her body on a piece of wreckage where, later, she regained consciousness.

When she and a few other survivors reached Wales, she cabled two words to her husband: "Saved alone." Taking the earliest available ship, he hastened to his wife's side, all the ache of his heart going out to her and to his Father God. It was when his ship reached the approximate spot where the *Ville du Havre* had met with disaster that God gave him the inspiration and courage to write:

> When peace like a river attendeth my way,
> When sorrows like sea-billows roll,

Whatever my lot, Thou has taught me to say:
  It is well, it is well with my soul.

*Lord Jesus, as You stilled the raging storm of the Syrian Sea,
so when my life is tempest tossed, speak Your word of peace and
calm.*

Portrait Eighty-four

INDIVIDUAL SONGS

God . . . gives songs in the night (Job 35:10).

God gave to Job different versions of songs in the night. We have considered the sublime songs of affirmation in Job 1 and 19. We have also meditated on the lyrical lines extolling God in nature and have in store God's own awesome anthem of creation He will give to Job. And, as we approach the end of his spiritual pilgrimage, we will hear further the divine accents and Job's own song of confession and triumph.

God works with us and in us as individuals. No two songs that He gives are the same. He composes a different score for every life and circumstance. He will give to you just the one you need to carry you through the darkness into the light.

One unique song came to Samuel Logan Brengle, the Salvation Army's great exponent of holiness. He was stationed in Boston when an incident occurred that cut short his career as a corps officer, or pastor, and very nearly finished him for a career of any kind. Having asked an unruly man to leave the service, and meeting with insolence and attempted violence in return, Brengle firmly ushered him through the door. The ejected one, however, waited his revenge. When Brengle appeared again in the doorway, the man hurled a whole paving brick at his ejector, striking Brengle's head full force.

For days, Brengle hovered between life and death. Following treatment, he was compelled to forgo active service for eighteen months. When the condition of his injury would allow, he devoted his time to writing articles for the Army's publication, *The War Cry*. These articles later were collected into a little red book, *Helps to Holiness*, which had a phenomenal sale, editions being published in many lands and in a dozen languages.

When someone would mention to its author how much blessing they had received from the book, Brengle would smile and say, "Well, if there had been no little red brick, there would have been no little red book."

One day Brengle found his wife painting a text on the brick. She had kept it, saying that she intended to make a collection of all the bricks with which her husband would be knocked down. The text she had chosen was that word from Joseph to his brethren who had sold him into Egypt: "As for you, you thought evil against me; but God meant it unto good . . . to save much people alive" (Gen. 50:20, KJV).

Another Salvationist, John Lawley, penned a song in the night from God:

> Though thunders roll and darkened be the sky,
>   I'll trust in Thee!
> Though joys may fade and prospects droop and die,
>   I'll trust in Thee!
> No light may shine upon life's rugged way,
> Sufficient is Thy grace from day to day.
>
> Thy word is sure, Thy promise never fails,
>   I'll trust in Thee!
> A hiding-place Thou art when hell assails,
>   I'll trust in Thee!
> I conquer all while hiding 'neath Thy wing,
> And in the storm sweet songs of triumph sing.

Heavenly Father, when shadows creep along the landscape of my life, unto the hills will I lift up my eyes and be assured that You are my Helper and will keep me from all evil.

Portrait Eighty-five

GOD'S WORD IN AFFLICTION

He speaks to them in their affliction (Job 36:15).

"God whispers to us in our pleasure," wrote C.S. Lewis, "speaks to us in our conscience, but shouts in our pains: it is His megaphone to rouse a deaf world" (*The Problem of Pain*, Macmillan, p. 81). God, in diverse ways, does speak to us in our hour of need. The words of Elihu to Job proved prophetic beyond his most daring imagining when he said, "But those who suffer He delivers in their suffering; He speaks to them in their affliction." As we soon will see, God will speak to Job with His longest recorded speech in the Bible.

Sometimes God speaks to us through the comfort and encouragement of friends. Sometimes He speaks through the circumstances themselves. Or we may hear Him through the inner promptings and enabling presence of the Holy Spirit who is the Paraclete, the One called alongside to help us.

Some years ago, my wife shared with me that she did not know how she could ever cope with the loss of her father, to whom she felt very close, when that day would come. It was not many years after our marriage that her father was stricken with a terminal illness and went to be with the Lord. Receiving word of his passing, we started out on the long journey home by car, hundreds of miles in the days before interstate highways. As we were driving through the night, she suddenly shared with me, "I don't understand it, but instead of the great dread that I feared, I have such a sense of peace." It was, of course, the presence and peace the Holy Spirit gives.

Our Lord, speaking to His bewildered and grief-stricken disciples on the eve of His crucifixion, promised, "I will not leave you as orphans; I will come to you" (John 14:18). The word translated "orphans" is the Greek word *orphanos*. In our hour of loss or suffering, God does not leave us as those without a Heavenly Father to comfort and help. Through the presence and power of the Holy Spirit, Jesus gives His great legacy to all believers: "Peace I leave with you; My peace I give you. I do not give to you as the world gives. Do not let your hearts be troubled and do not be afraid" (John 14:27).

Bishop Fulton Sheen, in his autobiography, writes of the blessings for which he was thankful, including the gift of Christian parents and opportunities for education. He then shares, "The greatest gift of all may have been His summons to the cross, where I found His continuing self-disclosure" (*Treasure in Clay*, Doubleday, p. 150). We too if we are attuned to His Spirit, will in times of cross-bearing hear Him speak His word of peace and strength and will know His continuing self-disclosure.

Dear Lord, thank You for the gift of the Holy Spirit, the gift of God Himself, to indwell my very life and enable me to cope with life's crises.

Portrait Eighty-six

HOW GREAT IS GOD

How great is God—beyond our understanding! (Job 36:26)

Elihu, in his oration, rose to poetic heights as he extolled the greatness of God. "God is exalted in His power" (36:22), he exclaimed and further praised: "How great is God—beyond our understanding!"

Some years ago, J.B. Phillips wrote a book entitled *Your God Is Too Small* (Zondervan). It identifies a weakness of modern man. We have become too glib, blasé about God. He has become "the man upstairs," perhaps viewed as a celestial Santa Claus. We tend to anthropomorphize God—to think of God in human terms and with human limitations. We need to recapture a sense of the awesome wonder and majesty of God.

It is a salutary experience of the soul to remind ourselves of His glorious attributes. The *Westminster Shorter Catechism* gives a distilled definition of God, using three adjectives, each of which applies to seven nouns: "God is a spirit, infinite, eternal, and unchangeable, in His being, wisdom, power, holiness, justice, goodness and truth." This summary statement embraces the omnipresence, omnipotence, omniscience, immutability, and eternity of God.

It staggers the imagination to contemplate these attributes in the context of cosmology, the study of the universe as a whole. For example, we are so geared to the finite that it is strange to think of God as an eternal, uncaused Being. Yet systematic thinkers are obliged to postulate some uncaused, eternal being in what is known as the *cosmological argument* for God, the explanation for the cosmos.

God is not only great as Creator but great in the magnificent design and intelligence of His creation. The *teleological argument* for God observes the intelligence, precision, and purpose in the cosmos. We live not in a multiverse but in a universe. There is harmony, precision, intelligence, order. Design postulates a Designer; intelligence postulates an Intelligence.

In systematic theology, there is also the *anthropological argument*, based on man's moral nature and sense of God. Job and countless others who have succeeded him discovered the greatness of God, not only in the might and magnificence of His creation, but in the stupendous expression of His love to mankind. This concept of "How great is God" is the theme of the song by Stuart K. Hine (Manna Music © 1953, used by permission) that has resonated its praise around the world.

> O Lord my God, when I in awesome wonder,
>   Consider all the worlds Thy hands have made;
> I see the stars, I hear the rolling thunder,
> Thy power throughout the universe displayed.
>
> And when I think that God, His Son not sparing,
>   Sent Him to die, I scarce can take it in;
> That on the cross, my burden gladly bearing,
> He bled and died to take away my sin.
>
> Then sings my soul, my Savior God, to Thee:
>   How great Thou art! How great Thou art!

Mighty God, I acknowledge Your sovereignty over the vast unending oceans of space and praise You with unspeakable gratitude that You stoop to reign over the lowly altar of my heart.

Portrait Eighty-seven

TREASURES OF THE SNOW

He says to the snow, "Fall on the earth" (Job 37:6).

Elihu, further extolling God's greatness, cited God's years as "past finding out" (36:26). As he contemplated the greatness of God, he was constrained to say, "At this my heart pounds and leaps from its place" (37:1).

Even the snow, said Elihu, testifies to God's greatness: "He says to the snow, 'Fall on the earth.' . . . So that all men He has made may know His work" (37:6-7). In the next chapter, God Himself asked Job, "Hast thou entered into the treasures of the snow?" (38:22, KJV) Again, something we tend to take for granted gives marvelous testimony of the craftsmanship of God.

God's handiwork is revealed in the exquisite geometry of the snowflake. He takes a globule of water, turns it from liquid to solid as it is suspended in air and forms a symmetrical, hexagonal design with infinite patterns. Of the incomputable number of crystals that fall to earth, no two snowflakes are alike.

Not only the form but the function of snow testifies to God's greatness. It serves the economy of the earth, blanketing the land and storing up moisture in the winter season. Not far from our personal retreat in the Catskill Mountains of New York State are large reservoirs that serve the water needs of metropolitan New York, over 100 miles away. Those reservoirs, and the millions of persons who take water from them, are dependent on two provisions—winter snows and spring rains. Each spring the deep blanket of snow melts and flows down the mountains into the streams and fills the great reservoirs. Without the winter snows, there would be a drought and a crisis for millions of residents. The *New International Version* renders God's question in words that seem to anticipate this provision for our times: "Have you entered the storehouse of the snow . . . which I reserve for times of trouble?" (38:22-23)

Sir Christopher Wren lies buried in St. Paul's Cathedral, the great church that his own genius designed and built. On his tombstone is a simple Latin inscription which means, "If you wish to see his monument, look around you." In a greater sense, if we wish to see the work of God, all we must do is look around us. His handiwork surrounds us, eloquently proclaiming His glory and greatness. And above all, His love is within us, proclaiming His grace.

Lord of the universe, I stand in awe and reverence before Your glory and greatness, Your mystery and majesty.

Portrait Eighty-eight
CONSIDER GOD'S WONDERS

Stop and consider God's wonders (Job 37:14).

In the midst of Elihu's eulogy on the greatness of God, he exclaimed: "Listen to this, Job; stop and consider God's wonders." It is good counsel to all of us, to pause and consider the wonders of God.

To stop is difficult in our culture. We are hyperactive people, traveling in the express lane, and we don't want to slow down, let alone stop. Our culture conditions us to quickness with its suntanning parlors, frozen-food dinners, McDonalds, Federal Express, Polaroid cameras, microwaves, and instant coffee.

But life constantly in the fast lane takes quite a toll. Our full-throttle lifestyle rapes relationships, substitutes frenzy for friendship, feeds the ego, but starves the inner man. A full calendar instead of a badge of success could be a symptom of failure in the things that really matter. Erma Bombeck asks, "Whatever happened to summer evenings when life was slower and you sat for hours on the front porch and listened to the swing squeak?"

Life in the fast-forward mode can keep us from an encounter with the wonders of God all around us. Like the sound of a distant bell comes God's call to man: "Be still, and know that I am God" (Ps. 46:10). It is a call in our day to beware of the barrenness of too busy a life.

From our ancient text of Job is sounded a note that needs to be heard above the fury and frenzy of our time. Let us "stop and consider God's wonders." We need to make ample room on our calendars for sunsets and stargazing, to ponder the tapestry of a tree and the delicate beauty and fragrance of a flower, to hear the carol of the birds, to walk through redolent pines after a rain, to look out on the vastness of an ocean, to feel the clasp of a friend's hand, and to see the quiet trust and love of a child's eyes.

God has fabulously endowed our world with wonders. Let us not go through life so fast that we will have missed them.

God of wonders, slow me down and open my eyes and mind and heart to Your wonderful world.

Portrait Eighty-nine

GOD SPEAKS IN THE STORM

Then the Lord answered Job out of the storm (Job 38:1).

The stage has been set for the grand climax of the drama of Job. We have followed the long orations of Job's four friends and the soul-searching responses of Job himself. Now, as the curtain goes up on the next to final act, God Himself appeared on the scene.

God addressed Job in His longest recorded discourse, comprising 126 verses of almost four full chapters. It is one of the most grand passages of the Bible.

Job had repeatedly expressed the wish that God would grant him an audience. In the biblical language of theophany (appearance of God), *Yahweh* comes to him "out of the whirlwind" (38:1, KJV). The *New International Version* reads, "Then the Lord answered Job out of the storm." God still comes to His children in the storms of their lives. When the winds blow fiercely on us and the storm rages within, above its roar we may still hear the whisper of His grace.

A personal encounter with a tragedy that seared our hearts eloquently witnessed to this truth. Three-year-old Joel Knaggs was struck by an auto and not expected to live through the night. His parents, highly respected Christian youth leaders, and their beautiful family were immediately embraced in a network of love and prayer. A prayer vigil by their Salvation Army church home was immediately set into action. Medical staff attending Joel gave not only their skill but shared their own Christian faith and compassion. But little Joel's head injury never allowed him to regain consciousness. With their own son's death imminent, Captain and Mrs. James Knaggs ministered to another couple in the hospital waiting room who were going through crisis. Also, the decision was made to donate Joel's organs so in his passing he would give the gift of life to another child. The young woman driver of the car which had struck Joel became an object of concern and ministry.

At the hospital, in the moments of anguish just following release of the apparatus that had sustained Joel, Captain Knaggs shared with me that he and his wife sensed the comfort and reinforcing presence of the Holy Spirit. The wound was deep and excruciating, but the whisper of God's grace was being heard above the raging storm.

The climactic moment came when, on a rainy Monday morning, close to 1,000 persons came from all walks and stations of life and gathered for what was termed "A Celebration of Love." The music, message, and prayers of Joel's funeral brought expressions of love and trust in God. And, in the tender moments at the end, those present moved through a long procession to express their love and support—through a word, a handshake, a hug. No words can describe the sacred scene, the sense of the Spirit's presence and ministry. It was a transforming experience, indelibly etched on the soul.

Yes, when the heart is breaking, and it seems we cannot go on, He will whisper His words of comfort and strength. And that will enable us, as we will see with Job in the end, to turn even catastrophe into celebration.

God of comfort, when the storm clouds gather and the shadow of sorrows falls across the threshold of my life, enable me to be so attuned to You that I will hear the whisper of Your grace.

Portrait Ninety
IN THE SCHOOL OF SORROW

Then the Lord answered Job out of the storm (Job 38:1).

"Where is God when it hurts?" asks Philip Yancey in his insightful book by the same title. He then answers with some of the ways that God reveals Himself in the storms of life: "He has promised supernatural strength to nourish our spirit, even if our physical suffering goes unrelieved. He has joined us. He has hurt and bled and cried and suffered. He has dignified for all time those who suffer by sharing their pain. He is with us now, ministering to us through His Spirit and through members of His body who are commissioned to bear us up and relieve our suffering for the sake of the head. He is waiting, gathering the armies of good. . . . Then, He will create for us a new, incredible world. And pain shall be no more" (Zondervan, 1977, pp. 182-3).

Biblical and secular history are replete with examples of God speaking to His children in the storms of life. Not only has God spoken to them, but He has spoken through them. We can never compute the debt the world owes to sorrow. Most of the psalms have come to us out of the crucible of suffering. The messages of the prophets were often proclaimed out of trouble and travail. Most of the Epistles were written in prison. Study the lives of the greatest poets and you discover they "learned in suffering what they taught in song." From Bedford jail, God spoke immortal words to the world with *Pilgrim's Progress*. And what of the prophets and poets of our day, such as Joni Eareckson Tada, Corrie ten Boom, Aleksandr Solzhenitsyn, Charles Colson?

Many who have trod the path of suffering and sensed the Presence on the road will share the sentiment of the unknown poet:

> I walked a mile with Pleasure,
>   She chatted all the way,
> But left me none the wiser
>   For all she had to say.
>
> I walked a mile with Sorrow,
>   And ne'r a word said she,
> But, oh, the things I learned from her
>   When Sorrow walked with me!

Thank You, Lord, that when I walk my Emmaus Road, troubled and disquieted because someone precious has been taken away, Your presence will flood my prosaic path with Your peerless glory and turn my Good Fridays into Easter Sundays.

GOD'S UNANSWERABLE QUIZ

I will question you, and you shall answer Me (Job 38:3).

A well-known television commercial announces, "When E.F. Hutton speaks, people listen." At the time of this writing, Hutton has developed some legal hassles, and not as many listen to him now as previously. But when God speaks, as Job discovered, man listens.

God bombarded Job with a fusillade of questions, seventy of them. He plied Job with rhetorical questions to which Job pleaded ignorance. When God was finished with His quiz, Job's score was zero!

In the divine-human encounter, Job heard the Creator of the universe challenging:

> Who is this that darkens My counsel
>   with words without knowledge?
> Brace yourself like a man;
>   I will question you,
>   and you shall answer Me (38:2-3).

God's speech to Job was expressed in unsurpassed poetic beauty as He unveiled His glory in the wonders of inanimate nature. He cited, as examples of His majesty and mysteries, the wonders of the earth, dawn, sea, light, weather (38:8-20). These common phenomena are mysteries of nature that elude the understanding of man.

In this passage, we find one of the most intriguing revelations about God. We should not be surprised that the God who created the playful cat and the funny-looking camel, and who bestowed a hearty laughter in the heart of man, has a sense of humor. God's humor was revealed as He chided Job, saying: "Surely you know, for you were already born! You have lived so many years! (38:21) Perhaps geologists and astronomers more than anyone will see the hilarity of God's statement!

In one of the memorable lines of Job, God asked him, "Where were you . . . while the morning stars sang together and all the angels shouted for joy?" (38:4-7) Job remained speechless before God's probing quiz. He was mute before the imponderables of God's creation. The story is told of a scientist who was asked to state his summary of the universe in 150 words. He responded by writing fifty times the words, "I don't know." Job did not even try to answer God's questions about the Creation and the universe.

How grateful we are that God's greatness transcends our ability to know and understand. For if my finite mind could grasp the infinite God, then it would bring God down to my human level.

And the miracle of miracles, that Job did not know but we can, is that this mighty Sovereign became my Saviour!

God of glory, thank You that we mortals can "join the mighty chorus which the morning stars began."

Portrait Ninety-two

DEATH'S INTRUSION

Have the gates of death been shown to you? (Job 38:17)

In the midst of God's litany of the wonders of His creation, we find the intrusion of death. God asked Job, "Have the gates of death been shown to you?" The question seems out of place amid the mysteries and majesty of the universe. We in the editorial profession would have labeled it for deletion or repositioning as a *non sequitur*. But God confronted Job with the reality and mystery of death among the riddles of the universe. Job, who himself was on the threshold of death, again was without an answer.

Life indeed is fragile, and death has a way of intruding when least expected, at the most untimely, unsuitable, and unsettling times. Our country was traumatized by a dramatic illustration of this. On January 28, 1986, the soul of our nation was stirred and seared as we saw the feathery flame explode from the spacecraft *Challenger* and our courageous astronauts vanish into the fiery nightmare.

Aboard the spacecraft was schoolteacher Christa McAuliffe, who had caught the imagination and won the heart of America. Going into space as the first nonprofessional, she represented so much of what is good about America. She ventured toward the heavens with her son's stuffed frog, her daughter's cross, her grandmother's watch, and a lesson she had ready to beam back to her classroom in Concord, New Hampshire. Not long before the ill-fated launch, she took time to write to encourage a Salvation Army Sunday School in Manchester, New Hampsire. She congratulated them on their theme, "Discovering New Frontiers," and wrote, "Since I am embarking on one of my own right now, I know how exciting that will be for you. Sometimes we get stuck with what is comfortable and we don't want to venture into the new." Christa McAuliffe was to venture to the ultimate frontier of humankind—beyond the gates of death.

A noisy high school auditorium of celebrants in Concord suddenly became hushed. With them a nation was stunned by the horror of the seventy-three-second ride to catastrophe. With them, and families of the seven who had dared to break the bonds of earth, a nation wept. We watched as our President led our nation in mourning. It was like a death in the family.

In the aftermath of the tragedy, we had to be impressed with a profound truth. Life is fragile. It can be snuffed out in an instant. On that day in January, the world watched as death defied even the almighty computer and all the technology man could amass.

The answer to the question put to Job, "Have the gates of death been shown to you?" had to await the triumphant resurrection of Christ. He answered the question for all of us: "I am the resurrection and the life. He who believes in Me will live, even though he dies; and whoever lives and believes in Me will never die" (John 11:25-26).

Christ, our risen Lord, I praise and thank You for Your resounding answer to the riddle of death. Because You rose and live, I can face tomorrow and eternity.

THE CELESTIAL WATCHMAKER

Can you bring forth the constellations in their seasons?
(Job 38:32)

God next recited the wonders of His stellar spaces. His celestial constellations are not objects of happenstance, but are governed by "the laws of heaven" (38:31-33).

It is mind-boggling to consider what astronomers tell us about the cosmos. For example, a galaxy is composed of billions and billions of stars. There are some 100 billion galaxies, each with, on the average, 100 billion stars. Our Milky Way, that scintillates over us on a clear, dark night, contains some 400 billion stars of all sorts moving with a complex and orderly grace.

We are told that a handful of sand contains about 10,000 grains. Carl Sagan states that "the total number of stars in the universe is greater than all the grains of sand on all the beaches of the Planet Earth" (*Cosmos*, Ballantine, p. 196). With Immanuel Kant, we are constrained to be filled with awe by "the moral law within and the starry heavens above."

Suppose a man finds a watch in a remote desert. He picks it up, examines it, and observes it is a complicated and crafted mechanism. He notes that the whole instrument functions with a perfect precision. He sees further that it tells the time of day, the month and year, has an alarm, and other intricate functions. He concludes that such a watch, with its design and precision, must have a watchmaker. Intelligent design presupposes a designer; order presupposes an intelligence.

We live in a world of infinitely more intelligent design and order than anything made by man. The precision of the universe is such that man can predict an eclipse within a fraction of a second, years in advance. Such design must have a Designer. Such intelligence must have an Intelligence. Such a world must have a World-Maker.

In His words to Job, God was revealing what Job needed most to know—who God is and His sovereignty over all things, including man. When we have a proper concept of God, then we will know we can trust Him. That will make all the difference.

Poet E. Ruth Glover has beautifully expressed this passage of Job in her poem, "A Family Affair":

Who shuts the mighty sea with doors?
Who opened gates of death?
Who is the Dayspring from on high?
Who gives life by His breath?
Who sees the treasures of the hail?
Commands the eagles' view?
Who is the Father of the rain,
And who begets the dew?
Who from His chambers waters hills?
Whose springs run to the valley?
From whose womb cometh forth the ice?
Who keeps the stars by tally?

And should my world spin uncontrolled,
Or should dark stormclouds gather,
When He who runs the universe,
I know as loving Father?

Mighty and wonderful God, help me to know that the God who holds the galaxies and stars in His hands is One to whom I can safely trust my life and needs.

GOD'S MAGNIFICENT MENAGERIE

Who provides food for the raven when its young cry out to God? (Job 38:41)

In the next part of His quiz for Job, God unveiled His glory in the wonders of animate nature. In vignettes of peerless poetry, God flashed on the screen of Job's imagination unforgettable word pictures of His magnificent menagerie (38:39–39:30). It has been described as "a passage that could be addressed to the Sierra Club or the Audubon Society" (*Where Is God When It Hurts?* Philip Yancey, Zondervan, p. 82).

God's amazing creatures parade before the awestruck gaze of Job. First there are the stalking lions, then the mountain goats and deer in the mystery of their birthing, and delightful portrayals of the wild donkey and wild ox. Next the ostrich, though admittedly stupid, is so fleet of foot (it has been clocked at sixty miles an hour) as to mock the horse and its rider.

The war horse, the only domestic animal in the discourse, is described in classic terms. The monarchs of the air—the hawk and the eagle—with the rest, display the unique and beautiful endowments of the Creator. This text could well be the basis of the hymn by Mrs. Cecil Frances Alexander, written for children:

> All things bright and beautiful,
> All creatures and small,
> All things wise and wonderful,
> The Lord God made them all.

God's lesson to Job was that if Job could not understand the providence of God as revealed in the natural world around him, how then could he understand the higher spiritual realm of providence in God's ways and care for man. Job had wondered where God was amid all the suffering of the world. Now he was led to see that God was all about him, if only he would take time to look. He had been so preoccupied with himself that he was missing God's revelation in every corner of the universe. Now God had illustrated that in the economy of His universe, nothing happens apart from His knowledge and power.

Job was constrained to confess his ignorance before God: "I am unworthy—how can I reply to You? I put my hand over my mouth. . . . I will say no more" (40:4-5). When we consider the providence God has endowed in the animate world about us, we can learn a powerful lesson of God's care for us. Jesus used one of God's creatures to teach such a lesson: "Look at the birds of the air; they do not sow or reap or store away in barns, and yet your Heavenly Father feeds them. Are you not much more valuable than they?" (Matt. 6:26)

Father, whose eye is on the sparrow, I thank You for the assurance that You care for me.

Portrait Ninety-five
THE BEHEMOTH
AND LEVIATHAN

Look at the behemoth (Job 40:15).

God gave Job an educational warmup with Zoology 101. Now He was ready to introduce Job to two of His most extraordinary wild beasts. A major portion at the end of God's speech described the *behemoth*, believed to be the hippopotamus, and the *leviathan*, thought to be the crocodile (40:15–41:34). They are portrayed in exaggerated poetic imagery.

There is surely a lesson to learn from God's portrayal of the bizarre behemoth. David L. McKenna brings out an illuminating insight on this "riddle of creation" as described in our text. He points out that "the hippopotamus is ugly and useless . . . a ludicrous creature." But he adds, "Beauty and function are not the conditions of God's grace. . . . To judge the value of persons or events on their utilitarian merits is another dangerous doctrine . . . there is some of the ugly and useless in each of us." He cites this bizarre creature of God's creation as "a precious example of God's grace" (*The Communicator's Commentary—Job*, Word, 1986).

The second of these two extraordinary creatures described by God was the *leviathan*. In romantic poetic imagery, it was described as intractable, invincible, fierce, formidable, and fearless with "nothing on earth his equal" and "king over all that are proud" (41:33-34). The leviathan is symbolic of Satan and evil.

Through this imagery, God revealed a dynamic concept that

sheds light on the universal problem of suffering. There is, with Satan, a monstrous and powerful evil force in the world. Many will know the anguish of his ferocious attacks, as did Job. But, as revealed in this discourse, God is sovereign of the universe and all things are under His ultimate control. He may allow suffering, but in the end, He will bring forth justice and judgment.

God has allowed Planet Earth to be Satan-occupied territory for a season. But there is coming a day when all evil and suffering shall be vanquished and righteousness and peace shall reign.

Help me, Lord, on my pilgrim pathway, to know that I journey toward the eternal city where there will be no more sin or sorrow and where deepest joys shall never cease.

NOT WHY, BUT WHO

My ears had heard of You but now my eyes have seen You (Job 42:5).

Any glib and facile answers to trouble and tragedy just do not ring true in a world where headlines scream of starving millions, suffering refugees, the searing inhumanity of the Holocaust, and the nuclear nightmare that menacingly haunts every new generation.

Robert Frost's lengthy and delightful poem on Job, "A Masque of Reason," presents a dialogue in heaven after Job's earthly experience. God says, "Oh, I remember well: you're Job, My patient." He further says to Job:

I've had you on My mind a thousand years
To thank you someday for the way you helped Me
Establish once for all the principle
There's no connection man can reason out
Between his just deserts and what he gets.
Virtue may fail and wickedness succeed.
'Twas a great demonstration we put on. . . ."

Indeed our finite minds cannot fathom the reasons for the testings and trials of life. But we can trust the sovereign God to bring ultimate purpose from our pain, and triumph from our trials.

Sixteen times Job had hurled to the heavens his anguished question, "Why?" But God never answered the question *why*.

Fifty-nine times we encounter the word "who" in reference to God. And that simple change of a "y" to an "o" is what made all the difference. It is what gives the Book of Job its message to us today.

Job did not need to know why. He just needed to know who—who was in control; who cared for him; who would sustain and vindicate him.

The great message and life lesson that comes to us from this ancient book is that we do not need so much an explanation of God as we do an experience with God.

To the matchless and magnificent message of God, Job replied: "I know that You can do all things." He admitted he was talking of "things too wonderful for me to know" (42:2-3). It was now a new Job who declared: "My ears had heard of You but now my eyes have seen You" (42:5). He had taken the quantum leap from hearsay to firsthand experience with God. His preoccupation with *why* gave way to a submission to and trust in *who*.

No longer protesting his righteousness before a holy and just God, he confessed: "Therefore I despise myself and repent" (42:6). Though he had not been guilty as his friends had accused, he needed to repent of his presumption and complaints before God.

He was vindicated by God, who three times referred to him by the same ascription as in the Prologue (1:8), "My servant Job" (42:7-8). The battle is won. Job did not denounce God as Satan had predicted.

Heavenly Father, help me to be open to Your self-disclosures, not merely to know about You, but to know You as a reality in my life.

Portrait Ninety-seven
GLIMPSING GOD'S GLORY

But now my eyes have seen You (Job 42:5).

Job knew one of the rarest experiences of humanity. He had a personal encounter with God. In one of the privileged theophanies of the Bible, those appearances of God to man, Job heard God speak to him and was able to say, "My ears had heard of You but now my eyes have seen You."

We cannot gaze directly at the sun or we will be blinded. The Bible tells us that man cannot look on the glory of God and live. God has to filter His glory for us to catch but a glimpse of His ineffable splendor.

Moses had prayed, "Show me Your glory" (Ex. 33:18). But mortal capacity has its limits. Man could not look on the flaming splendor of the infinite God. The great lawgiver, huddling in the cleft of a rock, had to be content with but a glimpse of the burning skirts of One whose power is flaunted by orbiting spheres and who is eternally clothed in majesty and holiness and before whom suns are but as candles and stars as jewels in His diadem.

Job discovered, as have others, that when you see God, you also see yourself in a different light. Isaiah, in his awesome vision of God, became overwhelmed by his uncleanness and cried out, "Woe to me. . . . My eyes have seen the King, the Lord Almighty" (Isa. 6:5). Ezekiel, vouchsafed with a vision from God, fell prostrate to the ground (Ezek. 1:28). Daniel, who lived one of the most perfect lives in the Bible, collapsed and fainted when God appeared before him (Dan. 8:17). John, as recorded in the last book of the Bible, upon seeing the ascended and reigning Saviour, "fell at His feet as though dead" (Rev. 1:17).

When God came to Job, his ash dung heap became an altar as he poured over himself the charred remains of his pride, saying, "Therefore I despise myself and repent in dust and ashes" (42:6). It is only as we come to truly know God that we come to truly know ourselves. Only in the light of His presence and glory do we see ourselves as we really are. Before Him all our pretense and illusions vanish, and we see our unworthiness, our pride and sin, and what we will become by His grace.

Marlene Chase has written, "At the apex of suffering it seems that nothing really helps . . . that all that is left to do is lie in the dust of our dead dreams. But then the warm breath of God comes upon us and we can hardly believe the subtle surprise upon waking that we are whole again." Job came to a new and deeper awareness of God and experienced a wholeness he had not known before.

The same breathtaking opportunity awaits every believer. Today we can glimpse the glory of God as Job never could. We can know within our lives the One of whom John testified: "The Word became flesh and lived for a while among us. We have seen His glory, the glory of the one and only Son, who came from the Father, full of grace and truth" (John 1:14).

Lord, lead me to higher aspirations, grant a glimpse of Your glory that I may go on from vision to victory in Christ.

Portrait Ninety-eight
RECONCILIATION

After Job had prayed for his friends, the Lord made him prosperous again (Job 42:10).

Job's friends had falsely accused him. They had insulted him and cast invectives against his integrity. We read in the final chapter that after the Lord had spoken to Job, He said to Eliphaz, the elder statesman among Job's friends, "I am angry with you and your two friends, because you have not spoken of Me what is right" (42:7). He required of them a sacrifice and told them that Job would pray for them. He accepted Job's prayer and did not deal with them according to their folly. Job's friends repented, no doubt confessing their wrong against him. Job prayed for them "and the Lord accepted Job's prayer" (42:7-9).

The account then reads, "After Job had prayed for his friends, the Lord made him prosperous again" (42:10). This passage has some deep life-lessons for us to glean.

It speaks to us of the need for forgiveness. To be unforgiving is to be unforgiven. Only when Job had prayed for those who had rubbed salt in his wounds did he himself find God's forgiveness and wholeness.

This passage also speaks to us of the need and power of intercessory prayer. How reassuring it is to know that our love for others is not powerless in their hour of need.

The text also reminds us that our own healing comes in part from our reconciliation with others. It was *after* Job had prayed for his friends that he experienced restoration. The

Lord calls us to be instruments of reconciliation as well as to be reconciled where there may be a division, an estrangement, a misunderstanding.

Can we not imagine the joyful embrace that took place between Job and his former contestants, perhaps with a locking of arms as they walked away together from Job's ash dung heap to the great feast and celebration described. It is one of the most felicitous experiences recorded in the Bible, with the reunion of family and friends and each one bringing a gift of friendship (42:11).

Help me, Lord, in all my relationships, to know the healing of forgiveness, the joy of reconciliation, and the ministry of intercessory prayer.

Portrait Ninety-nine

RESTORATION

The Lord blessed the latter part of Job's life more than the first (Job 42:12).

The familiar happy ending reads, "The Lord blessed the latter part of Job's life more than the first." Everything he had formerly owned and lost was now doubled: his sheep, camels, oxen, donkeys, and even his life span is twice the proverbial "three-score and ten."

However, in the description of the doubling of Job's assets is one of the beautiful serendipities of this book. God did not double the number of children Job formerly had. At the outset, he had seven sons and three daughters (1:2). At the end, he is given seven sons and three daughters (42:13). Here we have a precious intimation of immortality. For, unlike his material possessions, his children were not "lost." They had gone on to the larger life God has for those who belong to Him.

What a comforting assurance lies hidden in the numbers of this felicitous paragraph on the blessings of Job. Any who are bereaved of a beloved child, take heart! They are not lost. They are in His care, and someday there will be a grand reunion.

"To suffer passes; to have suffered never passes." The pain will one day cease. But what we learn in the time of trial is our treasure forever. Misfortune never leaves us where it finds us.

More important than Job asking the question, "Why did this happen?" was to discover, "Where will it lead me?" Job in his suffering was led to a deep discovery and awareness of God that surpassed all the treasures he had lost. And it is from his trials that we have this magnificent book. If life had flowed along smoothly for Job, there would have been no Book of Job with its radiant insights and inspiration.

God enables us, through His grace, not to waste our sorrows. Joni Eareckson Tada triumphantly testifies out of her paralysis: "His grace enables me to rejoice, not in spite of my disability, but because of my disability. God has a way of reaching down and wrenching good out of it. God aborted Satan's scheme in my life and brought good out of it."

What happens when bad things happen to good people? Through the grace of God, they become better people, and God turns their sufferings into servants for His glory.

God of the Book of Job, help me to know that it is better to walk with You in the darkness than to run in the light alone.

Portrait One Hundred
THE ULTIMATE ANSWER

Let us fix our eyes on Jesus . . . who . . . endured the cross. . . . Consider Him . . . so that you will not grow weary and lose heart (Heb. 12:2-3).

The Book of Job reveals our home as the stained planet, a fallen world. C.S. Lewis reminds us, "We are living in a part of the universe occupied by the rebel. Enemy-occupied territory—that is what this world is" (*Mere Christianity*, Macmillan). But the Book of Job eloquently teaches us that God is the Sovereign of the universe. He is in control. He cares for us and sustains us in our trials.

John R.W. Stott amplifies this truth from the perspective of the cross: "Sometimes we picture God lounging, perhaps dozing, in some celestial deck chair, while the hungry millions starve to death. . . . The cross smashes to smithereens this terrible caricature of God. We are not to envisage Him on a deck chair, but on a cross. The God who allows us to suffer, once suffered Himself in Christ, and continues to suffer with us and for us today. The cross of Christ is the proof of God's personal, loving solidarity with us in our pain" (*The Cross of Christ*, InterVarsity Press, 1987).

Job himself can be considered a prototype of Christ. As we experience Job's journey of faith, we see the pages rustling with radiant parallels of our Lord. A series could well be developed on the parallels of legendary riches, blameless life, temptation, impoverishment, affliction, rejection, faithfulness, restoration, intercession for reconciliation.

It is when we, who live in the New Testament era, come to

the One who has suffered above all others that we find in the Wounded Healer the grace for our trials and tragedies. Christ is the ultimate answer of God. He is God's supreme articulation for the otherwise meaningless riddle of suffering. Our Lord leads us beyond the shadows of Gethsemane and the darkness of Calvary to the glorious dawn of the Resurrection and to life eternal with Him.

Charles W. Carter, eminent Bible scholar, presents an insightful summary on this monumental book: "To solve the problem of suffering is not the supreme purpose of the author of Job. The book does not give us an answer to that problem. Rather, its first and prime purpose is to show that unselfish devotion to God without regard to temporal benefits, and in spite of human calamities and sufferings, is possible for those who know God intimately and have faith in Him for Himself alone. . . . The book teaches unequivocally that true religious faith in the person and integrity of God will win out in the end" (*The Wesleyan Bible Commentary*, Volume II, Baker, 1968, p. 21).

The counsel from Bunyan's *Pilgrim's Progress* beautifully summarizes much of the message from the Book of Job: "And I said to the man who stood at the gate of the year, 'Give me a light that I may tread safely into the unknown,' and he replied, 'Go out into the darkness and put your hand into the hand of God. That shall be to you better than a light and safer than the known way.' "

Annie Johnson Flint's beautiful verses make a fitting conclusion to our study of this priceless book:

He giveth more grace as our burdens grow greater,
   He sendeth more strength as our labors increase,
To added afflictions, He addeth His mercy,
   To multiplied trials, He multiplies peace.

When we have exhausted our store of endurance,
   When our strength has failed ere the day is half-done,
When we reach the end of our hoarded resources
   Our Father's full giving is only begun.

His love has no limits, His grace has no measure,

His power no boundary known unto men;
For out of His infinite riches in Jesus
He giveth, and giveth, and giveth again.

Thank You, God, for the Book of Job, for its precious insights and inspiration that will serve as landmarks for my pilgrimage of life.